SAVING ABIGAIL

THE TRUE STORY OF THE ABDUCTION AND RESCUE OF A THREE-YEAR-OLD HOSTAGE

LIZ HIRSH NAFTALI

Post Hill PRESS

A POST HILL PRESS BOOK
ISBN: 979-8-89565-022-6
ISBN (eBook): 979-8-88845-947-8

Saving Abigail:
The True Story of the Abduction and Rescue of a Three-Year-Old Hostage

Cover design by Conroy Accord

This is a work of nonfiction. All people, locations, events, and situations are portrayed to the best of the author's memory.

Post Hill Press
New York • Nashville
posthillpress.com

Published in the United States of America
1 2 3 4 5 6 7 8 9 10

In loving memory of Smadar and Roee

This book recounts my personal memories and experiences. I have made every effort to ensure accuracy while relaying this traumatic time with urgency, in the hope that it will bring attention to the plight of the hostages and help free our loved ones.

1

The shrill monotone of Tel Aviv's air-raid siren woke me up on Saturday, October 7, 2023, a little before 6:30 a.m. Seconds later, an announcement rang out across the Hilton in English and Hebrew, directing guests to the stairwells immediately.

The Hilton Tel Aviv is a 1960s high-rise that still dominates the north end of the two sun-kissed miles of broad beaches that make up the front yard of Israel's largest and most vibrant city. In the view from my upper-floor window, the center of the Jewish state's energetic culture and high-tech economy seemed as untroubled as on any other early weekend morning during the pleasantly mild days between summer and the rainy season. Runners were racing down the seafront promenade while the day was still cool, and a few early-rising swimmers bobbed in the gentle morning tide of the Mediterranean. I headed for the stairs.

The stairwell was mainly crowded with religious people who had been preparing to leave for synagogue, along with a few of us who were still in pajamas. It was not only Shabbat, an observant Jew's mandatory weekly day of prayer and rest, but also Simchat Torah, the annual celebration of the completion of the yearlong public reading of the first five books of the Bible. The early risers among the religious were as intent on cultivating their relationship with God as the runners outside were devoted to perfecting their bodies.

I had arrived in Israel the evening before, just as Shabbat began. My daughter lived in Jaffa, a mixed Jewish-Arab neighborhood a mile and a half down the coast from the Hilton. It is one of Tel Aviv's leading arts neighborhoods and the site of the oldest continually operating port on Earth. I wondered whether she had also heard the siren. Was she also in a stairwell, somewhere not so far away?

There was still very little to see when I returned to my room after the danger had passed. Everything below me looked calm. A single air-raid isn't enough to shock Israelis out of their normal lives. Tel Aviv might be the only major city in the developed world where bomb sirens are routine enough to be almost unremarkable. Some Tel Avivians have come to ignore them entirely. After all, the Israeli-developed Iron Dome interceptor system had proven to be astoundingly good at shooting down enemy rockets, at least so far.

I'm up already, I thought. Might as well take my morning walk. I changed into workout clothes and headed downstairs. By 7 a.m., there was already a decent-sized crowd on the promenade getting an early start to a gorgeous holiday morning. It certainly beat staying in the hotel room.

I'd walked a couple hundred yards down the coast when the siren sounded a second time. There is a parking garage beneath the section of the promenade next to the Hilton—Tel Avivians know how to find the nearest shelter almost by instinct, and I found thirty other people underground, waiting the customary minutes until they were sure the incoming rocket had been intercepted. By the third siren, which sounded a few unnervingly short moments later, I realized it might be a good idea to head back to the hotel.

This is eventually going to stop, I was still thinking around 7:45 a.m., with only a creeping sense that "this" might in fact be something out of the ordinary. In Israel, there can be rockets in Sderot in the south or Metula in the north; meanwhile the dancing in Tel Aviv continues, and the cafés only empty out when the siren rings—and sometimes not even then. On their own, sirens in Tel Aviv, although rare, don't automatically indicate a nationwide crisis underway. I had an 11 a.m. brunch date with my daughter. There was no reason to believe we wouldn't still make it.

These were the last moments in which it was possible for me to believe that something brutal and life-changing wasn't happening—that the sirens weren't announcing a wrenching, immediate break in our prior lives. In reality the world we'd known had already come apart, whether we knew it yet or not.

I was back in the stairwell around 8 a.m. after yet another siren, huddling for safety with the Orthodox Jews dressed in their best holiday clothes and clutching their tallis bags. Religious Jews are not allowed to use their phones on Shabbat or on certain holidays. But already we were hearing whispers and feeling the dread of an onrushing nightmare.

Something was happening an hour's drive south of Tel Aviv, along the border with Gaza. It was a part of the country where some of the most formative moments of my life had happened. I still had family down there, in a village of eight hundred people called Kfar Aza. Three generations of relatives lived on this kibbutz, which is the Hebrew term for a community where members hold common ownership of the major businesses and collectively provide for many social needs. My family in Kfar Aza ranged in age from my sister-in-law Shlomit, who is in her seventies, to my great-niece Abigail, who was just three years old.

When I returned from this latest trip to the stairwell, I called Shlomit, who didn't answer—it turned out she was in Bulgaria, on a trip with other older members of the kibbutz, though I didn't learn this until later. I then called Leron, one of Shlomit's four children. She still lived in Kfar Aza, as did her sister, the quiet and brilliant Smadar, the mother of Abigail and two other young children. Leron didn't answer either.

What was going on? Perhaps I somehow had the wrong number, I thought, my mind shielding itself against the crashing wave of disaster as long as it possibly could. Next, I called Nira, my other sister-in-law in Herzliya, a coastal city north of Tel Aviv. She was the family's kind-hearted gossip. She'd know if something was happening. She picked up the phone, and before I could say anything, she blurted out in pained Hebrew: *Smadar and her husband Roee have been murdered, along with their baby Abigail.*

***

Israel is not a foreign country to me. I lived there for a decade between the early 1990s and early 2000s. All four of my children went to nursery and elementary school there, on Kibbutz Shefayim, near our longtime home. My time in Israel covered a period of remarkable growth, possibility, and chaos for the world's only majority-Jewish country. Living there through a once-hopeful peace process with the Palestinians and through the frequent terrorism that followed turned me into someone who could adapt to the best and worst surprises, and who could also sense the potential hidden behind every obstacle. The story of what Israel means for me, and of how it achieved its many real yet fragile successes amid violence and insecurity, can be told through my Israeli family, the ones who were being slaughtered and hunted as I sat frozen, alone in a Tel Aviv hotel room, barely able to breathe.

My former husband is an Israeli who was born in Baghdad and moved to Israel with his family when he was six. After Israel's founding, Iraq's Jews, who in the early twentieth century formed a quarter of the capital's population, were given the "option" of emigrating to the new Jewish state. In exchange for letting them out of the country, the government would confiscate all of their property. Nearly all the Jews of Iraq made the decision to leave, following a period of lethal discrimination.

Iraq had been a home to Jews for over 2,500 years, since the Babylonian destruction of the first temple in Jerusalem when they were forced into exile. For millennia, Baghdad served as a historical center of Jewish intellectual life. But in 1941, on the Jewish holiday of Shavuot, an outbreak of violence known as the Farhud erupted in the city against Jews. This became a turning point in the history of the Jews in Iraq. By the late 1940s and 1950s, as these state-encouraged mob attacks on synagogues and Jewish neighborhoods became common, and as communal leaders were put on trial for the crime of being Jewish—in 1948, one prominent Iraqi Jew, Shafiq Adas, was hanged in front of twelve thousand spectators in Basra—it became clear that this history had come to an end. Jewish history had also ceased in the ancient communities of Syria, Egypt, Libya, Saudi Arabia, Yemen, and other Arab countries. Within a few years, almost all of the more than one million Jews of the Middle East, many of whose families had practiced their religion and ancient trades for centuries and even millennia prior to the birth of Mohammed, were either formally expelled from their home countries or forced to leave under duress.

My mother-in-law, Marcel, fled Baghdad after a failed arranged marriage, and she landed at the kibbutz, whose communal lifestyle helped her as a refugee and single mother to three children. There she met her second husband, Shabtai, an American who attempted to move to Israel after his service in World War II. Before he made Aliyah, he went to France to help Holocaust survivors board boats for the holy land. By the time he was finally ready to make his own way to Eretz Yisrael, the British were blockading all Jewish immigration into Mandatory Palestine. He wound up in a British detention camp in Cyprus, a place filled mostly with refugees who were Holocaust survivors, people who had lost their homes and families in the slaughter of Europe's Jews. Shabtai finally arrived in Israel and followed his dream to live on a kibbutz. Shabtai was a widower, and Shlomit was the only child from this previous marriage.

My husband, one of Marcel's three children from her first marriage, was a real estate developer living in Los Angeles when I met him. The end of the Cold War opened up new and exciting opportunities in Israel, which was emerging from a long spell of economic and diplomatic isolation. Peace with Jordan, the Palestinians, and maybe even Syria was just around the corner. The country's long experiment with socialism was nearing its end. The economy was primed to take off, and Israelis would soon have the money, and the consumer tastes, for American-style shopping malls. My husband and I moved to Israel after we were married. We raised five children there and spent the 1990s and 2000s building one of the country's leading chains of retail centers.

I was prepared for such an ambitious and hard-charging project—just as I was prepared for the more intense ways of life in a country that I'd only visited twice before moving there. Hard work and a sense of connection to the wider world were part of my upbringing. My mother's father was born in Harbin, a freezing Siberian city, once part of the Czar's vast empire, now part of modern-day China. After a few years making gyroscopes during his service in the US Navy in Corpus Christi, Texas, my father, a native New Yorker, started successful businesses in clothing manufacturing, real estate, and retail in the Los Angeles area, where I was born.

My parents both came from modest backgrounds, and they put me to work selling clothes and collecting rent when I was thirteen. They also taught me to care about other people. In the '70s and '80s, both of my parents were active in the movement to pressure the Soviet government into giving millions of Jews the right to emigrate to Israel, where they could safely practice their religion. They donated to Jewish and social justice causes. Through their involvement in anti-poverty charities in LA, they taught me that Jews weren't only supposed to care about other

Jews: we had a social responsibility toward all of our fellow humans.

My parents also had an eye for political talent. One of the first politicians my father supported was an Arkansas governor who didn't know much about the Jewish people living in LA, a guy named Bill Clinton. My father thought he was very bright and was happy to assist. My parents also became friendly with Joe Biden when he was an unknown senator from Delaware in the early 1980s.

Still, there's only so much that prior experience can prepare you for when it comes to life in a new country, especially one as peripheral as Israel was in the early 1990s. In 1992, Tel Aviv's skyscrapers were at least a decade in the future. Israel wasn't yet a high-tech economic miracle. The mail and even the phones were notoriously unreliable, and the country had maybe a single Chinese restaurant. McDonald's only opened there in 1993. I remember standing in line at the post office for hours to pick up a small package sent from the US, only to be told I had to go to the bank to pay import taxes on its contents before they could release it to me. This was typical: a range of basic services required visits to multiple offices whose only purpose seemed to be to waste everyone's time.

Then, as now, you had to be determined, and even a little bit harsh, to make it in Israel. You quickly had to learn that the first answer to any question will often be "no," and that this "no" will likely be followed with a gesture-heavy lecture about how wrong you are. You also had to learn that an Israeli "no" doesn't always mean "no." It is a cherished part of the national character to make things harder than they need to be, at least at first. But once you've stuck up for yourself, once you've pushed enough to break the other person's façade of determination and pushiness, most Israelis would rapidly drop their hard outer shell, and they'd turn out to be some of the warmest people on Earth.

I tried to follow my parents' example in Israel. I established a fund within our real estate company that supported children in underserved communities and underwrote programs that brought the country's Arabs and Jews together, as well as helped the absorption of recent refugees from Ethiopia. I believed in peace between Israel, the Palestinians, and every country in the Middle East, and not only because Yitzhak and Leah Rabin would often be on the neighboring court at our tennis club in Herzliya. Israel is small enough that the war-hero, peacemaking prime minister and his wife could play as a husband-wife doubles team against the citizens they governed. Rabin would personally greet everyone on the courts, run after every ball, and yell whenever he messed up a shot. When he was assassinated in 1995, murdered by a Jewish extremist opposed to the peace process, I thought it was the end of the world.

It was my Israeli family that helped me ground myself in this new country, which was so unfamiliar and bewildering. My husband and his family were not religious, but life in Israel moves according to the rhythms of the always-crowded Jewish calendar even for avowedly secular people. While Orthodox Israelis dedicate their Saturdays to religion, many of their less observant compatriots spend Shabbat with their extended families. Many families, like ours, got together just about every weekend without ever praying or setting foot in a synagogue.

Many times, we made the hour-and-a-half drive from Herzliya to Kfar Aza, following the coast and then heading east into the edge of the Negev desert. The kibbutz was nestled amid the meadows and hills next to the Gaza Strip, which was then controlled by Israel. There was no high-tech border fence in those days, and no real sense of a nearby lurking menace. Palestinians from the Strip worked on the kibbutz often without incident, crossing the border to get to their jobs each day.

My first memories of Kfar Aza were of an Israeli paradise. Fields of bell peppers carpeted the plains at the base of the green, gentle hills. Everyone knew each other; children roamed around without their parents having to worry about anything—my own kids loved climbing on the strikingly simple playground equipment and petting the cows at the kibbutz's dairy farm. Three generations of a family would live in the same neighborhood, and children would wander into their grandparents' houses whenever they felt like it. We spent many weekends and holiday afternoons in the little garden outside my sister-in-law Shlomit's home, eating watermelon and feta cheese and drinking hot tea.

The kibbutz had a plastics factory and eventually developed a successful live-event production business—diversification that explained how Kfar Aza stayed viable at a time when other such communities were losing residents. Sixty years earlier, the entire area had been an uninhabited desert. Amid the pines and eucalyptus trees, it was impossible to imagine a time when Kfar Aza had ever been barren—before it blossomed into its own warm, self-contained world. I loved going there.

I especially loved it there because of Shlomit, Shabtai, and Leron. Leron was a little girl in the early 1990s, but she spoke English incredibly well for a non-native speaker of any age. My Hebrew wasn't fluent yet, and Leron helped me connect to other members of my husband's sprawling family of Israeli-Iraqi-American kibbutzniks. Leron's brother Nimrod was a sporty young adolescent, who, a decade later, would be badly injured in combat in 1996 while fighting against Hezbollah in Lebanon. The eldest sister, Gilat, a beautiful heavily eye-lined teenager, eventually moved to London to raise her family.

Their sister Smadar was much younger and quieter than everyone else. When she grew up she was always articulate and very kind, and when she spoke you knew there was a keen intelligence behind her somewhat shy outward appearance. As an Arabic-fluent professional within Israel's vast national security apparatus, she wound up in a position where a sense of discretion was a requirement.

Smadar married Roee, a professional photographer who worked for some of the country's biggest newspapers and websites. They had three children: Michael, Amalia, and little Abigail, who was born in 2019. All of her children were born long after Israel made a complete withdrawal from the Gaza Strip in 2005, a move that was widely embraced by the international community following the horrors of the Second Intifada, and that even most Israelis saw as a necessary, difficult step towards long-term peace and security. In 2007, Hamas took over the coastal territory from the ruling Palestinian Fatah party in a short but bloody civil war, not long after winning what are still the most recent Palestinian legislative elections. Peace did not arrive, neither for Gazans nor for their Israeli neighbors.

Over the course of Smadar's life, the field behind the kibbutz became a militarized border, with a hostile jihadist enclave ruling the nearby coastal plain. Attacks by Hamas and other Palestinian terror groups on Kfar Aza became so frequent that children could tell the difference between a rocket and a mortar just by listening. Kids too young to walk on their own knew to hop into the nearest adult's arms when the alarm sounded so they could be carried quickly to safety.

Smadar and her family lived in a new neighborhood in Kfar Aza—from their front door you could see through an ever-more sophisticated-looking security fence to the boxy concrete fringes of the Gaza City sprawl, just three-quarters of a mile in the distance. It was impossible to live in Kfar Aza while remaining totally naïve about the risks of doing so.

The same could be said for all of Israel: the dangers were evident, and well beyond what citizens of any Western nation would remotely accept as normal. At the same time, for Israelis, they seemed manageable. Most days were quiet, and Israel was home—the only home Israelis had.

Despite the rocket attacks and the occasional military conflicts with Hamas that followed, most of which lasted a few weeks, the people of Kfar Aza did not consider the Gazans their enemies. The kibbutzim around the Gaza Strip were populated with people who believed in coexistence with the Palestinians: They voted overwhelmingly for secular, pro-peace parties and welcomed Gazan workers into their communities every day. The kibbutzniks would often volunteer to drive Gazans to hospital appointments in Israel.

They could not ignore the dangers of their surroundings, though. More than once, Smadar grabbed the kids and drove to her in-laws' home further north when she had suspicions that a bigger-than-usual attack could be coming from Gaza. Like the rest of Israel—including the country's military, intelligence, and political leaders—she went to bed on the night of October 6 believing that nothing out of the ordinary was happening.

***

Hamas attacked Israel in overwhelming numbers early in the morning on October 7, 2023, with an estimated force of three thousand terrorists breaching Israel's borders by land, sea, and air. Commandos from the group's elite Nukhba Force arrived at Kfar Aza in pickup trucks and landed near the center of the village using fan-powered paragliders. They smashed through an apparently worthless border fence with trucks, tractors, and construction equipment and crossed the fields on foot. In total, an estimated 200 to 300 terrorists overran a place in which perhaps 650 people were physically present. Most of Kfar Aza's residents were asleep when the assault started.

The active first line of the Kfar Aza volunteer security force totaled about fifteen people, most of whom were unarmed. The close connection between Kfar Aza and Palestinians in Gaza meant that Hamas was already well acquainted with the layout of the village and its security operations. The invaders knew where the kibbutz armory was, and they killed several volunteers as they darted to retrieve their weapons. By mid-morning, one in every ten residents in Kfar Aza would be dead or in terrorist captivity.

Smadar and her husband Roee, along with their children—nine-year-old Michael, six-year-old Amalia, and three-year-old Abigail—lived on the corner of the kibbutz that was closest to Gaza. People in Kfar Aza live so close to the Strip that they see and hear rocket fire long before any sirens go off.

A little after 6:25 a.m., Roee grabbed his camera and went outside, not yet knowing that terrorists were invading his own community. His photos of the beginning of the bombardment—terrorists hang-gliding into the kibbutz; and thousands of rockets, missiles, and mortars fired from Gaza, all part of the largest such single-day assault against Israel in the country's history—were later published on the website of Israel's largest newspaper, *Yediot Ahronot*. By 6:30 a.m., the entire family was awake. Meanwhile, the trained Hamas commandos had begun methodically fanning out across the kibbutz, going house by house and killing or kidnapping whomever they could find.

Hamas terrorists barged into the house while Roee was still out photographing the rocket attack. They were wearing fake olive-green IDF uniforms, made in a Hamas-controlled factory in Gaza City. Smadar was among the first in Kfar Aza to die. She was shot in front of her three small children as she rushed to secure them in their reinforced safe room. It is impossible to imagine what it was like for Michael, Amalia, and Abigail to see their mother murdered in front of them in the middle of their home, especially with their own lives in danger, with bullets flying all around and killers closing in. The three children rushed out the door.

As they left the house, they saw their father running towards them. He had heard the direction of the gunshots. Roee grabbed Abigail in his arms. Michael and Amalia darted beside him. Shots rang out.

The children watched as their father fell to the ground on top of their baby sister. The terrorist who killed Roee looked Michael and Amalia in the eye, and in the unthinkable terror of the moment, the children ran towards the greatest safety they knew. They sprinted home, climbed over their mother's dead body, piled into a closet, and hid there in the dark, alone.

Michael and Amalia called Shlomit from the darkness of their closet to tell their grandmother what they had seen. When they reached her in Bulgaria, she didn't believe them at first. She needed proof before she could start processing the fact that she now lived in a world where her daughter had been murdered: She asked the children to leave their closet for a moment and show her their mother's body on video. They gave their despondent grandmother the grim certainty she said she needed during the worst moment of her long life. They also told her that their father was shot dead, and that they thought Abigail was too.

Back in the closet, a chain of anguished phone calls to friends and family eventually led Michael and Amalia to a social worker who lived in the north of Israel. For hours, this person went to heroic efforts to keep the children company on the phone, to calm them down and serve as a lifeline to a steadier world. From the dark closet, Michael asked this woman who they would live with, as he knew his parents were dead. She assured them that everyone would want to take care of them because they were smart, beautiful children. At one point, the children's phone was nearly out of battery, and the therapist had a hard decision to make: Was it worth one of the children risking their life to leave the closet and retrieve a charger? Was it worth the price of making them see their mother's body again? She decided that hours of agitation, loneliness, and fear, along with an inability to communicate with the outside world, were much more dangerous to Michael and Amalia than spending a few quick moments outside their hiding place. She was scared of what would happen if she lost touch with these children. Michael quickly, bravely fetched a charger and returned to the cramped darkness.

Help wasn't on the way yet. It wouldn't be for a while. The Israeli army and police were so overwhelmed, and caught so off guard by the assault, that it would be fourteen hours until Israeli special forces made it to Kfar Aza and found the children in their closet. They were confused, terrified, and shattered—but physically unharmed and alive.

***

Smadar's sister Leron lived on the other side of Kfar Aza with her husband Zoli, a burly Hungarian-born chef and restaurant owner, and their three kids. By 6:30 a.m., Leron and her family knew that terrorists had infiltrated the kibbutz. The kibbutz's WhatsApp groups started lighting up with eyewitness accounts of what was happening around them. By 6:35 a.m., a picture had emerged out of the quickening avalanche of text messages: a mass invasion was underway, an event of a kind that no one on the kibbutz had ever seen before.

These real-time channels offered people immediate, often excruciating, windows into what was happening around them, but it also saved lives. Leron and Zoli quickly shut off the house's air conditioning, turned off all the lights, unplugged major appliances, and hid the family in their reinforced safe room. When terrorists came in and out of the house throughout the day, they believed that the inhabitants were out of town. If Leron and Zoli had been less fastidious about concealing their presence, they might have suffered the same brutal fate as their murdered neighbors.

In a continuation of the day's general pattern of complacency and wishful thinking, it turned out that many safe rooms in the kibbutz, designed for rockets, couldn't withstand a terrorist invasion. In Kfar Aza, Hamas terrorists succeeded in breaking into them—either because they didn't have locks, or because they could easily be shot off. Then they murdered or kidnapped whomever they found inside. No one was completely safe anywhere. Early that morning, a young woman knocked on the door of Leron's house after Hamas had murdered her husband. She carried her one-month-old daughter with her. Leron's family took her in, despite the danger that a crying infant could present. They couldn't turn these people away—they would find a way to survive the onslaught together.

One of the founding ideals of the state of Israel is that with a sovereign state behind us, Jews would no longer have to cower like hunted animals behind locked doors. Together, these seven people spent twenty-nine hours hiding before help finally arrived. It would be several days before Israeli forces secured Kfar Aza enough that the bodies of its murdered residents could be removed and buried. Roee's killers dragged his body hundreds of feet to the border fence. At that point, they decided that getting back to the Strip alive was more important than having another Israeli corpse to ransom, and they abandoned his body.

***

Back in Tel Aviv, I frantically called my Israeli in-laws. By noon I had pieced together that shortly before her murder, Smadar had been able to call her elderly father to urge him to go into his bomb shelter as soon as possible. I heard about Michael and Amalia's heartrending call with Shlomit, during which they also told her that their father had been murdered and that they believed their sister Abigail had been killed as well. I learned about the massacres on other kibbutzim, places like Be'eri and Nir Oz and the Nova music festival, where Hamas's killing had rivaled the Kfar Aza atrocity.

All morning and into the afternoon, I felt my throat clench. The air tasted sour; every breath was laborious and uncomfortable. I was not in denial—bad news has a way of creating its own new reality, and I am the kind of person who knows better than to fantasize about my experiences not being real. Instead, I was at the mercy of a disembodying shock, deeper and more profound than anything I'd ever felt before, the shock of not being able to absorb what you're being put through. I kept looking at the beach and the streets below, searching for signs of life. The swimmers and joggers were all gone. Traffic barely stirred. The modern world's first and greatest Jewish city remained hauntingly vacant the entire sunny Shabbat day.

I did not shut down, though. Even in the stupefying first hours of the tragedy, I realized there was something I could do. I could tell people what was happening and raise awareness of the atrocities unfolding in Israel.

I was in a unique position to tell the world about Hamas's cruelty. By coincidence, New Jersey senator Cory Booker had been on my flight to Israel the night before. I was currently splitting time between California and New York, where two of my children live, and the senator across the Hudson was a friend of mine. In fact, he had invited me to join him for Simchat Torah services and a holiday dinner at his friend's house in Jerusalem immediately after the flight landed the night of October 6.

Senator Booker has been close with the Chabad-Lubavitch movement ever since his days as a Rhodes Scholar at Oxford, which is how I had found myself, the night before the greatest attack on Jews since the Holocaust, attending services at an Orthodox synagogue for the first time in my life.

It was anything but dour or oppressively traditional: I danced and hugged the Torah with religious women, while across the room the senator and other men danced with their own ornately decorated scroll. We shot each other amazed glances, astonished that we were celebrating Simchat Torah in Jerusalem together in such a joyous way.

Israel can be a divisive issue in America, especially on the political left. Against the pressure of left-wing, anti-Israel voices who see him as a sellout, as well as right-wing, pro-Israel voices who see any sign of moderation as proof of insincerity, Cory Booker has a deep and real affection for the Jewish state, as well as a commitment to its survival and safety. I know that he feels its joys and tragedies personally. He wants a just outcome for Israelis and Palestinians and a region that can live at peace—which was the impetus for his trip, which started in Israel but was scheduled to move on to Ramallah and the Gulf Nations.

I should say here that I have long been active in Democratic Party politics, eventually becoming one of the party's deputy finance chairs after the 2016 election. I didn't dedicate my time and money to the party to gain favors from the powerful but for the much greater satisfaction of being able to find and encourage true leaders with the courage to approach big issues like reproductive rights, social welfare, and Israel with the empathy and understanding they require. To me, Senator Cory Booker has been a paragon of heart and humanity in an American political climate where Democrats and Republicans too often treat their opponents as if they're subhuman enemies.

To the extent that I have thought of myself as a political partisan or as a person with any real power, October 7 changed that too. At around 9:30 in the morning on October 7, I called Cory in Jerusalem. America is a country of 350 million people, and only a small number of them have the ability to call the personal phone of one of the country's one hundred senators. On the one hand, I am extremely fortunate to be connected to some of the top political leaders in America. On the other hand, one's sense of privilege tends to melt away when one's family is being murdered and hunted. In Kfar Aza, it was the people with guns and grenades who held the power when it really mattered.

Whatever impact I thought I had over anything didn't seem to matter now. Perhaps it had never mattered. This whole situation belonged to a world I didn't live in. A mass invasion of well-armed jihadist terrorists committing atrocities and broadcasting them in real time had never happened in Israel or any other developed, democratic country. My family had been victimized by something so awful that it couldn't even be imagined until it actually happened.

Booker answered my call. I told him everything I knew so far. He was stunned and silent, which is unusual for a politician as thoughtful as Cory.

I never really got dressed on October 7. As the day went on, images of burning, horror, and murder took over the news media and my phone. No healthy mind could process it all.

It was even more impossible to consider what this real-time orgy of mass sadism, murder, and rape meant for people I loved and knew intimately. There were no cameras on what was happening to each of my family members just ninety minutes down the road. I had no images, outside my imagination, of Leron and seven others crammed in a room, or of Michael and Amalia cowering in a small, dark closet feet away from their mother's body. Knowing that any of them could be murdered at any moment was more than I could handle.

In a daze I wandered up to the Hilton dining room. The religious Jews were still dressed for the holiday, which ended at nightfall. A buffet was set out—it felt to me like the deck of the Titanic. I am a vegan and wasn't sure what I could eat. I saw a mother with her young daughter and burst out crying when it reminded me of Smadar and Abigail. I sobbed to a hotel server that my family had been murdered. She hugged me and brought over tahini and pita bread. In the twilight the beach and the empty city looked menacing and gave off no comfort in its dreadful stillness.

I did not sleep at all that night, or the night after. Calls and texts came in from my family, personal friends, and those in the political world who knew I'd been in Israel or who had learned of my family members, murdered or in lethal danger. Senator Jacky Rosen and former House Speaker Nancy Pelosi checked in on me and offered their condolences and support. I was grateful, of course, but even their concern added to the larger feeling of unreality. Maybe it would make more sense tomorrow. Maybe it never would.

I traveled back to New York in a total fog. I don't really remember being in Dubai, where I had a layover. I felt as if a truck had hit me but that I was somehow still walking. The closest I could get to something approaching physical or emotional relief was to doze off, only to jerk awake and think: I can't believe all of this is real.

I do remember stopping at my daughter's apartment in Jaffa on my way to the airport. We just sat in bed, not saying much, not knowing what to say or do really. Just being together holding each other was enough. She was not leaving. Her place was in Israel, and she had lived in the Jewish state for her entire adult life. It wasn't yet clear what I could do, other than tell people the story of two children witnessing the killing of the rest of their family. As far as I knew, three-year-old Abigail was dead, murdered in her father's arms.

At that point, I didn't think there was anyone to save.

2

The emotional fog that set in the morning of October 7 followed me back to New York. Shock overwhelmed everything else. Time crept forward and events flashed by. Nothing could move me past the moment when I'd learned my family had been murdered.

I came home from the airport and spent a day crying in my apartment and making absolutely no progress at putting reality back together. I cried constantly during those early weeks, whenever I wasn't in a meeting or giving an interview. I've never cried so much in my life. I had never before reached that point where the tears felt like they had run dry, even though the crying wasn't over and might never be over. I kept feeling as if I couldn't catch my breath, like I was slowly and constantly suffocating.

An important insight emerged out of this waking nightmare, one that helped stabilize a world that never spun completely out of control for me, no matter how bad things got. In the most hopeless and confusing days after October 7, I began to realize I had something I could do. I could tell people what had happened. I could let people know what Hamas had done to my family, to Kfar Aza, and to the entire country. This could be important work, because the denial of the October 7 atrocities began that very day. The IDF was still battling for control of communities on the Gaza border when anti-Israel activists started claiming that most of the Israeli dead were soldiers, or that most of the civilians had been killed by the IDF, perhaps on purpose. It didn't matter that Hamas had recorded the attacks on GoPro cameras, making this the best-documented terrorist assault in history. By mid-week, the first credible reports of rape and sexual assault by Hamas fighters emerged. Anti-Israel activists dismissed these as a Zionist invention. Perhaps I could play a role in making sure the attack couldn't be erased from history.

From my apartment I could see the colossal glass façade of One World Trade Center, the tower that replaced the two skyscrapers where the deadliest terror attacks on American soil had occurred. I usually didn't think of death and fire and devastation when I looked out my window. In those days after October 7, it was all I could see: empty patches of sky where jihadists had murdered nearly three thousand Americans of every possible background. The world had been exposed as a violent, angry, and cold place, and it was as if cruelty and destruction now marked everywhere I looked.

A friend had a contact at CNN who arranged an interview on Abby Phillip's primetime show on my second night back in the US. Going to the studio and telling the story of the killings in Kfar Aza gave me an opportunity to share what had happened to my family. The idea that I could do something helpful offered me my first glimmer of hope.

I was still so devastated on October 10 that I have very little memory of that first television appearance. I was hesitant when the CNN producer asked me to share photos of Abigail for the camera. I wasn't sure it would help our family for pictures of the dead to be made public.

But in the green room was Carl Bernstein, the legendary reporter who helped break most of the major stories of the Watergate scandal, who was awaiting his own turn to go on the air. A journalist who had brought down a president looked increasingly broken as he listened to me explain what I was doing there. I showed him the pictures of my murdered relatives. He was stunned at learning that I was at the studio to talk about something so horrible.

His reaction helped me understand the power of being honest, even when it feels too painful to bear. If you confront people with the truth, they will remember you and will care about what you're saying, regardless of whether they're a senator or a famous journalist or a person without any power; their sympathies may matter in ways you could never imagine in the moment.

The fight for Abigail's freedom forced me to become an effective public communicator who could appear on television and speak with senior officials, sharing the story without blowing the moment or losing my nerve. A good story is something intangible and invaluable, but you have to learn how to use it properly.

In the middle of that first week, the story of what had happened to my family on October 7 changed completely.

***

I talked to my brother-in-law Dori every day the week after I returned to New York. The nine surviving family members from Kfar Aza, now refugees, had moved in with him and his family. He told me how Leron and Zoli had taken over the care of Michael and Amalia, their nephew and niece, in addition to their own three children. The family never hesitated in assuming responsibility for these young children, who had just lived through an enormous trauma. Just days earlier, Leron, Zoli, and their children had been hiding in dark rooms for twenty-nine hours awaiting rescue from terrorists. Now everyone was physically safe and provided for, at least those of our family members whom we knew to still be alive.

There were lingering questions about Abigail, though. Israeli forces had retaken Kfar Aza, but no physical sign of the young girl had been found anywhere on the kibbutz. It was possible a Hamas commando had taken her dead body to Gaza, but by that point there was already extensive footage of the Kfar Aza attack, much of it from the bloody GoPro videos that the terrorists themselves had filmed. None of this horrific footage showed the abduction of a three-year-old girl's corpse. The only evidence of Abigail's death was the eyewitness account of her two terrified siblings, who had seen their father murdered with their little sister in his arms.

October 7 was the one of best-documented mass-kidnappings in modern history. Hamas terrorists and the many Gazans who followed them into southern Israel—a group that suspiciously included photojournalists and videographers who worked for major Western media outlets, including the Associated Press and the *New York Times*—proudly filmed and even broadcast live their seizure of whomever they could subdue and drag off. The terrorists took whatever weak, vulnerable, terrified, or unarmed people they could round up, and treated them as spoils of war.

The terrorists didn't care if you were an elderly woman, like eighty-five-year-old Yaffa Adar, whom a gunman infamously carried off the Nir Oz kibbutz in her pajamas in a golf cart, or very young, like six-month-old Kfir Bibas. They didn't care if you were Jewish or not—Gazans dragged four members of the Bedouin Alziadna clan, all of them Arab and Muslim, back to the Hamas-ruled enclave. They didn't care if you were even Israeli at all: People taken hostage hailed from Thailand, Tanzania, Nepal, the Philippines, and numerous other places without a significant Jewish population or involvement in Middle Eastern affairs. The captives held citizenship from twenty-five countries in total, including the US, and included followers of at least five religions. The terrorists didn't even care if you were alive: at least a dozen of the eventual 246 hostages were murdered on October 7 and had their bodies stolen, with Hamas refusing to reveal which hostages were still living or not.

The hostages were not people who presented any threat to Hamas's governance in Gaza, an enterprise which has meant nothing but misery for Israelis and Palestinians alike. Israel's military and political leaders were not among the kidnapped. The hostages' strategic value to their captors was that they were human beings whom the terrorists could trade away or enslave or use as human shields or for psychological warfare.

For most of modern history, it has been reputation-wrecking for political groups to kidnap children, something that all decent people and the entire international community used to treat as automatic proof that a given organization was too brutal and evil to be trusted with anything, let alone control of the lives of millions of people. Child captives also have to be cared for in ways that adults do not. But Hamas quickly learned it could get away with inflicting ongoing national trauma upon Israel by keeping young Israeli children in captivity—and demanding that terrorists be released in exchange for these kids' lives and freedom. Hamas understood that children, like dead bodies, would carry a high price in any future negotiations with Israel.

Hamas kidnapped so many people from so many different locations that it took weeks, and in some cases months, to determine whether people were dead or in captivity. Hamas had touched off one of the worst hostage crises in modern times, one so massive that it was at first impossible to grasp its true scope.

Even the story of one little girl was full of heartbreaking ambiguities. There was no evidence that Abigail had died or had even been wounded. There was no body, but there was also no video of her being taken to Gaza. Hamas never confirmed Abigail was a hostage, because the group doesn't give away information about its hostages for free—they do so only if it can serve their aim of further terrorizing and demoralizing the Israelis, and even then, this information is unreliable. My family scanned every bit of gruesome raw footage from October 7 and every subsequent Hamas video, desperate to find any sign of Abigail. There was none.

What happened to her? When Dori first raised the possibility, on the Wednesday after the attack, that Abigail could be a hostage, it was just a hopeful hypothesis, though one that made logical and emotional sense to me.

Dori explained that, based on various accounts of the attack from survivors of the Kfar Aza massacre and from details that kibbutz members had learned over WhatsApp and the other messaging channels connecting their shattered but still tight-knit community, there was a strong possibility Abigail had somehow wound up at a neighbor's house after her father's murder. Hamas had later taken this neighbor hostage, along with her three kids. Dori said that an eyewitness at Kfar Aza had seen Hamas terrorists march this neighbor, Hagar Brodutch, off the kibbutz with her small children in tow. This person could not confirm if Abigail had been with them, Dori added.

I thought this news was reason for optimism. You can't really trust people's eyewitness abilities in the heat of a life-and-death situation. The witness could easily have mistaken Abigail for one of Hagar's children, or thought they'd seen three children when there had actually been four.

A couple days later, the information mill confirmed my deepest hopes and instincts. Hagar's husband, Avichai, had been one of the members of the Kfar Aza security team. In the event of an infiltration of militants from Gaza, he was supposed to throw on an olive-green uniform, leave his house, run for the communal armory in the middle of his kibbutz, and retrieve his weapon, a military-grade submachine gun nearly identical to the one issued to IDF conscripts. Avichai was one of the few who had made it to the armory alive. He fought the invaders, firing at commandos who had traveled a shockingly short distance to kill him, his neighbors, and his family—a journey of only a couple miles to the kibbutz's outer fence.

In the firefight, Avichai was injured badly enough to put him out of communication for a number of days. When he was in good-enough condition to share what he'd seen before he was shot, Avichai revealed the last thing he had done before leaving his family and sprinting for the armory: Abigail, his young son's friend and the little daughter of his best friend Roee, had shown up at his house, alone, frightened, and covered in blood. When he opened the door, he told us, Abigail ran away from him in fear. Avichai was in IDF-style army khakis, similar to the fake Israeli combat greens Abigail's parents' killers had worn. He caught up to her and picked her up in his arms. Avichai calmed the little girl down, put her in the safe room with Hagar and their children, and then left to defend his home—not knowing when or if he'd return.

Once we found out that Abigail could be alive, I became a new person. Now there was something to do. Now there was someone to save.

***

I had never met Abigail before. She was born in 2019, just before the COVID-19 pandemic made it impossible to visit Israel for a while. Now I would have to fight to ever get to see my great-niece. I would need to do whatever it took to make her freedom from Hamas a reality.

The campaign really got underway when I asked Dori if he had any new pictures of Abigail he could share. People would want to know what she looked like, and when they saw this adorable little girl, it would be impossible for all but the most depraved ideologues to believe she deserved to be a Hamas prisoner. I also wanted a picture I personally could look to for a sense of strength and purpose.

One image Dori sent was especially striking. I printed it out on a five-by-seven sheet and placed it on my desk in New York. In the picture Abigail sat on a red Persian rug at her house in Kfar Aza, a corkscrew of walnut hair covering her left eye. She looked directly at the camera and had the delighted, slightly conspiratorial grin of a child who knew she was up past her bedtime. Her small hands were curled over colorful building blocks and a pacifier. Her brown eyes were piercing.

My daughter wondered whether it wasn't too sad for me to see Abigail's sweet face every day and be reminded of what had happened, and was still happening, to her. In fact, seeing Abigail staring at me from across my desk stirred a deep inner resolve, an intensity of feeling I had never known and barely even recognized. The daunting task of rescuing Abigail from the clutches of terrorists was not something I had ever prepared to do, but once the situation presented itself, it wasn't something I could walk away from.

Working for Abigail's freedom wouldn't be easy. In the early days of the crisis, there was no formally organized effort among the families of the hostages. No one even knew how many hostages there were, or who they were. It was utter confusion. I had relationships and friendships in the American political world going back years and even decades, but it was unclear to me how or if their political pull mattered in a crisis as new and grotesque as this one.

Whenever I spoke to my sister-in-law Shlomit, she would ask if I could help save her granddaughter. I knew I had to do something. I could not single-handedly reverse the horrors of October 7, but maybe I could at least fix some part of a newly shattered world. And who knew what else would be possible once Abigail and the other hostages were free? I had a responsibility to act—and to do whatever was possible for the people I loved and cared about.

The week after October 7, I had an invitation to a small private event for a book by the actress Kerry Washington. I went during a time when everything was still a daze, and I just needed to get out of my apartment. At the event I ran into Huma Abedin, one of Hillary Clinton's top aides during her time as secretary of state. On October 7, Huma had heard I was in Israel and reached out to me to make sure I was safe.

At the party, we talked about what had happened to my family in Kfar Aza. Huma, who understands the inner workings of American diplomacy better than nearly anyone else I know (aside from Clinton herself), offered to help. When I told her that Smadar had American citizenship, Huma put me in touch with State Department officials to register her as a murdered American citizen—and, more importantly, to register Abigail as a missing American.

I had my own very small foothold in the world of American foreign policy. In 2021, I was nominated by Speaker Pelosi to the Commission for the Preservation of America's Heritage Abroad, a commission under the State Department with no formal power that focuses on the upkeep and creation of memorials and markers for Jewish and Holocaust-related sites in Eastern and Central Europe. I'd never asked to join the commission. In fact, I make a point of never asking politicians for anything. The only thing I've ever wanted out of my political engagement was to make America a better place. I was now in the awkward and unprecedented position of needing help from the political figures I knew.

From the beginning, it seemed possible to me that the diplomats, members of Congress, and Democratic Party activists who were part of my circle wouldn't be able to help Abigail. The post–October 7 hostage crisis was not only without parallel but was also fast becoming a global issue whose resolution depended in large part on the whims of Yahya Sinwar, the psychopathic Hamas leader who was believed to be in a tunnel deep under Gaza. If there was no immediate deal to free all the hostages at once—something that at the time felt possible—the direction of the coming war, and perhaps the fate of the hostages, would hinge on whatever decision Israeli prime minister Benjamin Netanyahu made about the method and scope of the response.

Freeing Abigail seemed an insanely ambitious goal most of the time. She was a part of events far bigger than the kidnapping and captivity of one tiny three-year-old child. There was nothing more important to me than saving her, but for the time being she was an objectively small part of a huge war. Over 1,200 Israelis were murdered on October 7. Over 240 more were kidnapped, dragged against their will across the border into Gaza, and held as hostages. Everyone went to bed on October 6 in one world and woke up in a new one on October 7.

Hamas's cross-border rampage had shattered every Israeli's sense of their own physical security and put the grief-stricken nation's strategic vulnerabilities on full display to its enemies and to itself. In that context, October 7 was not simply or even primarily another chapter in what Westerners had become habituated to calling the "Israeli-Palestinian conflict." Hamas was financed primarily by Iran—which, according to early reporting in the *Wall Street Journal* and the *New York Times*, had known of and approved Hamas's murder spree as part of its own long, slow, patient war against the Jewish state and the West.

The strategic situation in which Israel found itself had not been part of mainstream narratives even inside Israel, but it was now impossible to ignore for anyone attempting to understand the dynamics of the post–October 7 Middle East. Hamas had in no way been deterred from attacking Israel; in fact, they were a far more formidable force than Israeli or American leaders had understood, capable of crossing the border, taking control of multiple Israeli towns and military bases, and killing on a mass scale.

At the same time, Hamas was the least formidable part of the iron ring that Iranian leadership had been slowly tightening around Israel over the past decade. Iran had helped Hamas build its network of tunnels and rocket factories beneath Gaza. In the months before the attack, it had trained its elite Nukhba Force to fly paragliders over Israel's border fence. Hamas's capabilities were in turn dwarfed by those of Hezbollah, the Iranian-directed terror army, which had become the shadow government of neighboring Lebanon. Hezbollah boasted tens of thousands of soldiers hardened by fighting in Syria on the side of that country's brutal dictator, Bashar al-Assad, who had killed more than half a million of his own people. Hezbollah also boasted an arsenal of over two hundred thousand rockets and drones, which at any moment could set Israel's major cities ablaze and turn the north of the country into an uninhabitable wasteland. Secured in mountain bunkers inside Iran, beyond the reach of international inspectors, arrays of advanced centrifuges were enriching uranium to the levels required to produce nuclear bombs.

I am not a geopolitical expert. But, simply by reading the newspapers, it was clear to me that Israel had badly misread its surroundings. It was also clear that at any moment the situation of the hostages could easily get worse—a lot worse. If a new war with Hezbollah or even Iran broke out, as seemed entirely possible, millions of lives would be at risk—including Abigail's. And that was assuming that my three-year-old niece had even survived the opening phase of the fighting.

My game plan was simple: tell Abigail's story, to anyone and everyone. Tell it enough, and maybe the United States would step in and secure her freedom before it was too late. I believed that could happen, because I believe that America is a country that is capable of great things and that can accomplish nearly anything.

Practically speaking, I had no idea how to move the entire American federal government in the midst of an unprecedented geopolitical mess. But I knew that America was still the most powerful force on Earth, and that Abigail was an American. I knew that America still cared about its people, and when it focused its full powers towards a specific objective, it could make big things happen.

***

I saw Cory Booker again on Friday, October 13. The experience of being in the country on its worst day ever, during the deadliest slaughter of Jews since the Holocaust, had profoundly shaken him. That Friday evening was the beginning of the first Shabbat after October 7. Because the Torah cycle had restarted on Simchat Torah, the holiday that took place the day of the massacre, synagogues around the world would be reading the first chapters of Genesis, in which God creates the universe and humankind.

I accompanied Cory to services at Temple B'nai Jeshurun, a Reform synagogue in Short Hills, New Jersey. In his speech, Cory, nearly in tears, described his experiences in Israel less than a week before—the joy of dancing with the Torah that Friday night, followed by a Saturday-morning call from his chief of staff in the middle of an early-morning jog through Jerusalem, in which he learned that Israel was under attack. Cory spent the day in and out of bomb shelters, fielding frantic calls from Washington, President Biden, and me.

At B'nai Jeshurun, Cory channeled much of what Jews around the world were feeling in the days after the unimaginable. His voice cracked, and then dramatically regrouped, as he described what had happened to my family in Kfar Aza.

"There is no way to express the mountain of grief you can feel, the knowledge that you still didn't know all the evil that had been done—the stories coming out hour after hour, day after day," he recalled of October 7 to a crowd whose world had just entirely changed. He talked about Michael and Amalia cowering in a closet. Cory knew Abigail was being held hostage but had the discretion not to mention that yet.

That morning, he had Zoomed into a weekly Torah study with a rabbi he had long been close with. "The rabbi reminded me that it's a mitzvah to choose joy," said Cory, a believing Christian. In being commanded to seek the light even in moments of profound darkness, Jews have long understood that action is the best answer to despair. "The first time God speaks, He says, 'Let there be light,'" the senator said, quoting the week's

Torah reading. "It is our choice." He spoke about "the defiance of choosing joy, the defiance of being light to cast out darkness."

In the week after learning that Abigail could be alive, I woke up every morning confronting the sheer severity of the situation. Joy wasn't a possibility yet, but I couldn't let paralysis set in. I woke up many mornings thinking it was all a bad dream, with the reality not really hitting me until the day's first cup of coffee.

The first question that confronted me was whether talking about Abigail's situation, even in private, was actually a good idea. Common wisdom in government circles had once opposed the idea of families going public about their kidnapped loved ones, on the theory that publicity rewarded hostage-takers and incentivized future kidnappers. In the mid-2010s, the Islamic State of Iraq and Syria took several American hostages. The Obama administration told their families to stay quiet so as not to jeopardize negotiations or otherwise complicate the jobs of US government officials working for their family members' freedom. ISIS executed each of these hostages.

After Abigail's kidnapping, no one in the government knew what to tell me to do. No one told me not to share my family's story publicly. They told me to share if I thought it necessary, but I wasn't sure it was—or if it would help. What I did know was that one effective way to build up national awareness on a given issue is to go to Capitol Hill, knock on doors, and make a compelling case in person to whomever will listen—whether you imagine that they are on your "side" or not.

***

Later that month, I was committed to be in LA for the wedding of a lifelong friend's daughter and attend a baby shower in Malibu of my daughter's best friend. At the wedding, I watched small children, dressed in their finest, running around and laughing, and thought of Abigail. At the shower, I excused myself to Zoom in for an interview with Anderson Cooper.

These were happy occasions amid unbearable sadness—and then I had to put the happiness and the sadness on hold to go on national TV and plead for Abigail. The mental whiplash and incongruousness of it all were constant and exhausting. I had no idea who any of my appearances were really reaching, or if anyone was paying attention. But I felt obligated to do them.

As it happened, the interviews did have the effect of linking me to incredible people whose existence I would have otherwise never known about. One of them was a woman named Sophia Abram. A North Carolina-based investor in women's health startups and political activist, she was far beyond my New York–LA coastal radar. I am not sure how she found me. I had done a number of other media appearances the week after the Abby Phillip interview on CNN—I'd sleep-walked through an interview on Maria Shriver's podcast, back when I still thought Abigail was probably dead.

Abram called and invited me to join her the next day on Capitol Hill, where she was headed to advocate for American assistance to Israel during the crucial initial phases of the crisis—and also to press for the freedom of the 246 hostages, roughly a dozen of whom were Americans. Among those on the trip was the family of sixty-five-year-old Keith Siegel, another American hostage. I decided I'd join them. It was a chance to get the word out and to make sure lawmakers at least knew Abigail's name and face.

Abram might have lived in the South, but she knew how Capitol Hill worked. The group's many North Carolina connections meant that we got to meet both of the state's Republican senators, along with four members of Congress from both parties who represented the state. The night before, I'd gone to a print shop in Washington and made hundreds of copies of the photo of Abigail. I handed one to everyone I met on the Hill, no matter who they were.

While we were on the street outside the Senate office buildings, Abram introduced me to a tall Southerner with gorgeous blown-out hair, wearing a blue dress that was just a little too glamorous for a place as straightlaced as Capitol Hill. This was Penny Nance, a Liberty University–educated pastor's daughter and CEO of one of the country's leading right-wing grassroots organizations, Concerned Women for America. I have never been the kind of Democrat who carries on about the evil of the opposing party or its supporters. I am not a partisan attack dog. Still, activists like Nance have never been part of my world, and there are a range of issues, including ones I care passionately about, where we find little common ground.

Abram introduced me as the great-aunt of one of the youngest Hamas hostages. What is now a close friendship began with Nance praying for me and Abigail, right there on the street. She held my hand, closed her eyes, and quoted the Book of Jeremiah from memory: "A voice was heard in Ramah, lamentation, and bitter weeping; Rachel weeping for her children.... Thus, saith the Lord; Refrain thy voice from weeping, and thine eyes from tears: for thy work shall be rewarded, saith the Lord; and they shall come again from the land of the enemy." This lifelong Evangelical Christian recited a verse that recalled the hardships of one of the mothers of the Jewish people. I was blown away by Nance's commitment, her intelligence, and her ability to see the humanity in everyone. "There's a sweetness in the fact that we found common ground and something so much bigger than ourselves," she recalled when I hosted her on my podcast seven months later.

Nance empathized with my family's pain and wanted to do whatever she could to help. Our political disagreements and our differences in religion and background didn't matter—none of it stopped us from working together towards a goal that was bigger than ourselves. She is also a much sharper and more experienced political operative than I am.

I never would have dreamed I'd have so many nice things to say about a professional right-wing activist, but I couldn't fight for Abigail if I insisted on only speaking to Los Angeles or New York Democrats. The only way to succeed was to go outside my comfort zone and learn to understand and trust people that I might have dismissed or even stereotyped under different circumstances, or in an earlier phase of life. Nance helped change my outlook and reminded me there are people on all sides who draw from the same reservoir of common humanity. She also helped me find my way through the Washington labyrinth.

Washington is where America's elected representatives carry out the people's work, but it often doesn't feel that way. It's perplexing even for people who know what they're doing. With its broad avenues and stern marble façades, the capital often seems like it's hiding whatever its actual business is, or at least trying to keep the citizenry from snooping around too closely. Yes, it's true that, under most circumstances, just about anyone can still walk into any of the congressional office buildings and stroll around at their leisure. They can wander the interconnected basements and even ride Capitol Hill's internal subway system. But what's actually going on in the infinity of suites and conference rooms at a given moment is specialized knowledge that relatively few people possess.

A certain opacity is unavoidable: Members of Congress have extremely difficult and demanding jobs. Without layers of aides and other handlers, they wouldn't be able to master granular aspects of healthcare or agricultural policy while also handling the chores and rigors of an endless campaign cycle. I knew that Abigail's freedom depended on me being able to look people in the eye, hand them her photograph, and tell them her story. That also went for members of Congress, even the most idealistic of whom were likely, on any given afternoon, to be some combination of jaded, distracted, and overtaxed.

We met over a dozen members of the House and Senate, from both sides of the aisle, in a two-day sweep of the Hill. Bernie Sanders, Hillary Clinton's primary opponent in 2016, reassured me Hamas wouldn't kill Abigail—she was too valuable as a hostage for them to kill. Bernie is like a gruff, slightly grumpy grandfather, warm and bristly at the same time. His Republican Senate colleague Susan Collins, who Nance introduced me to, isn't on my political team, but she carried a picture of Abigail with her everywhere she went after I gave her the photo during our first meeting.

"I know you know that I'm not from your party," I told Collins. We first met after a meeting I'd had with six other Republican women who served in the Senate. Our eyes locked and we clutched each other's hands.

"That doesn't matter," the senator replied.

We never went into our many points of disagreement—we kept the discussion focused on a kidnapped child and her murdered parents. Senator Collins became one of Abigail's truly ceaseless advocates. She mentioned the three-year-old hostage at every opportunity, to anyone who would listen. On a bipartisan congressional delegation to Israel just a few days later, my daughter Noa tried giving Collins a picture of Abigail and was amazed when the senator pulled the one I had given her in Washington out of her purse. Later that day in Tel Aviv, Collins held up the photo at a press conference and told the world they were looking at the face of a three-year-old hostage in Gaza.

One of the more revealing meetings on the Hill was one that didn't happen in the end. I wanted to meet with members of the "squad," the far-left group of congressional Democrats, several of whom would come to openly side with Hamas in the post–October 7 war. But that wasn't a given back then, or so I thought. Perhaps the plight of the hostages, and the sheer evil of kidnapping a three-year-old child after murdering her parents, would make them second-guess their own worst instincts, lowering the temperature of a divisive party-wide and nation-wide debate.

I decided early on that I'd meet with absolutely anyone to push for Abigail's release. Late on Thursday afternoon, Sophia and I walked into the office of Rep. Rashida Tlaib, the Palestinian-American firebrand from Michigan. A young staffer was happy to meet with us. He and a colleague listened for twenty minutes as I shared Abigail's story. I gave him the picture of Abigail, as well as a second picture with the faces of every hostage. An hour after we left, he called Sophia and said that the congresswoman had already returned home for the weekend but would like to meet with us the following Tuesday.

Then, over the weekend, Tlaib sent a tweet declaring that Palestine would soon be liberated "from the river to the sea." It dawned on me that this person, who is a member of my own political party, did not believe in Israel's right to exist. In fact, Tlaib believed in the preferred violent end-state that was the motivation for Hamas's attack in the first place. Nothing about October 7 had made her reconsider her stance. In fact, she believed in the elimination of Israel more than ever. In the months that followed, she became one of the loudest and most passionate American voices promoting the psychotic ideological program of Abigail's jailers.

The congresswoman was of course entitled to her opinion. However, it also dawned on me that there were 434 other members of the House, and that it would be a better use of my time and emotion to meet with them. Saving Abigail was more urgent and worthy a goal than pleading with the Rashida Tlaibs of the world to have sympathy for a captive child.

***

Members of Congress deal with a million different things every day. In group settings their staffers are often frantically scrolling through texts and emails, putting out the day's fires and staying on the lookout for any new ones to stomp.

One of the keys to advocating on any issue is that, on some level, you have to treat everyone exactly the same. No matter who they are, you have to look straight at people's faces, both because it is hard for someone to be the first to break eye contact and because you can gauge their reactions as they are actually happening. Whenever I told Abigail's story in Washington and showed her five-by-seven photo, the room fell silent, except for the occasional sound of someone sniffling back tears. I was putting even the most hardened of the Hill's denizens through something heart-wrenching, something they couldn't ignore—something they'd remember. Something they'd act on.

I wasn't a stranger to a lot of people I met in Congress. They knew me as a fundraiser, a businesswoman, a loyal Democrat. But now they were also seeing a different me: someone who'd been made powerless by a terror group, and who desperately needed their help.

But they weren't just moved by seeing someone from their universe being flung so violently into a vortex of Middle Eastern conflict. It was the story itself that floored them. An orphaned young child was in a terrorist dungeon. Now, her physical and mental health, and the rest of her life, depended on what we could do to free her. When I looked around and saw how silent some of the least sentimental people in America were, I understood the importance of sharing this story.

That trip to the Hill was the first time I used a line that I'd recycle nearly every day for the next two months: *I need all of you to be Abigail's mother and father, and advocate for her.* Abigail's parents had been murdered, I told every member of the House and Senate that I met. I am doing my best to give her a voice, but I can't do this alone. Abigail needs all of you to do for her what her parents can no longer do. We are who she has now.

For at least a few minutes at a time, I could make it seem like Abigail's fate, and the fate of hundreds of other hostages, depended on what the listener said and did. Perhaps that was true in some limited way. Maybe it would become true once enough people believed it. But the situation in the Middle East was getting murkier and scarier by the hour. The war was gearing up, and the hostages' chances of survival were narrowing.

It took Israel nearly three days after October 7 to fully secure the territory around its border with Gaza. President Biden sent an aircraft carrier to the eastern Mediterranean, a masterstroke that successfully discouraged Iran's other local proxy groups, like Lebanon-based Hezbollah, from launching their own big attacks. Israel was reeling, but with the situation stabilizing, the country could begin mounting a counter-attack against Hamas. Biden had flown to Israel and promised America would stand by its ally amid its worst crisis in decades, but he also warned Israel not to repeat America's post-9/11 mistakes, and to mount a measured response that achieved something more lasting than mere vengeance would. Meanwhile, Hamas's spokesmen gleefully promised to repeat the atrocity "again and again" until Israel was destroyed.

Within a few days of October 7, Israel began the largest military mobilization in the country's history, calling up some four hundred thousand reserves to active service. Israel's stated purpose in any coming war was to recover the hostages, dismantle Hamas's military capability, and ensure that terrorists from Gaza could never threaten Israelis again. It was unclear how long such an operation would take, and how many Israelis and Palestinians would be dead by the end of it. It was anyone's guess if the hostages could survive what was coming. Hamas militants threatened to execute their captives on live television in the event of a ground invasion.

The hostages were almost certainly not being kept in a single location. Some were probably being hidden in plain sight, among civilian buildings and infrastructure. Others were in tunnels deep under Gaza's most densely populated areas. Later it would come out that some of the hostages had been kept in hospitals, where at least one of them was very likely executed. There was always the possibility that a sadistic Hamas member would abuse one of the hostages to death, or that an Israeli bomb would strike the wrong tunnel or building, accidentally killing some of the captives.

Worries about less tangible matters began gnawing at me. If this blameless little girl died in Gaza, she would be a footnote in a larger tragedy, and the century of conflict between the peoples of the Middle East would have denied her a future before she even had much of a chance to live. It was a race against time, with no way of knowing how much time was even left. As the war escalated, I would have to escalate my own efforts if Abigail was to have a chance at making it out alive.

3

If October 7 threw me into a numb state of shock, at least I wasn't alone. The same was true for people who held real power. Key leaders in the Middle East and elsewhere were unsure of how to respond to events that no one had anticipated. Israel began an intense aerial bombardment of terror targets in the Gaza Strip but lingered for weeks on committing to a ground invasion of the enclave. The Israelis had little choice but to respond forcefully to the large-scale massacres and kidnappings of innocent civilians inside the borders of their country, yet no one could predict exactly what form that response would take.

A nightmarish regional war was still an imminent possibility. On October 8, Israel was reported to have ordered fighter jets into the air to attack Hezbollah targets in Lebanon, only to have President Biden strongly advise Israeli prime minister Benjamin Netanyahu to recall the planes to their bases. Fearful of renewed Hamas attacks, the opening of a second front in

Lebanon, and ballistic missiles from Iran, hundreds of thousands of Israelis fled their homes in the north and south of the country. Abigail's kidnapping was morally outrageous and personally painful, but the lives of many more children would soon be in danger.

The gathering chaos clouded any clear path to freedom for Abigail. The coming war's devastation might soon overshadow any global concern for her fate, or for the lives of the other hostages. Having kidnapped Abigail and slaughtered her parents, along with over 1,200 other innocent people, 40 of whom were Americans, the Hamas murderers would now invite the sympathy of the world for their genocidal cause by retreating into the massive underground city they had constructed with foreign-aid dollars and by using the civilian population of Gaza as human shields. The hostages were human shields too—Hamas could use Abigail's safety, and the threat of her death in war, as a pressure point against its enemy.

I did have a number I could call for help, the one Huma Abedin had given me when I saw her in New York. It belonged to Roger Carstens, a diplomat and retired US Army Ranger who holds one of the more intense jobs in the federal government. Carstens is the special presidential envoy for hostage affairs, a role he assumed in March of 2020. The former lieutenant colonel is one of very few Trump political appointees whom Biden did not replace.

I first spoke with Roger Carstens by phone on October 19 and visited his office at the State Department in early November with my daughter Noa. I had been to the State Department's Foggy Bottom headquarters just once before, for the unveiling of Hillary Clinton's official portrait as secretary of state.

Carstens works at the intersection of the geopolitical and the personal. He deals with members of the American public at their most desperate, and his job is to use the prestige and abilities of the US government to even the power imbalance between the family of a hostage and whatever state, criminal gang, or terrorist group is holding their loved one. He deals with the most emotionally intense and politically sensitive issues, scenarios where both individual lives and the credibility of the United States are on the line. Failure is common, and the successes often remain secret.

Carstens strikes a reassuring figure. President of his graduating class at West Point and a veteran of six different US military campaigns, he has the short-cropped hair and strong jawline of a former military man who has spent a lifetime in the roughest parts of the world doing the most dangerous jobs possible. Yet there is also a palpable gentleness to him, a real feeling that he views you as a human being and won't stop fighting for you until every possibility has been exhausted.

Carstens was hardly sanguine about the challenges of freeing Abigail. His office had a wall displaying the pictures of hostages he'd helped bring home. I noticed portraits of victimized journalists, unlucky businessmen, bold religious missionaries, and the basketball star Britney Griner.

I also noticed that the gallery of photographs on Carstens's wall didn't include any pictures of three-year-old girls, or for that matter any children at all. On October 7, Hamas carried off thirty-two Israelis under the age of eighteen. The mass kidnapping of young children by terrorists was something few people in government—including, as it turned out, senior officials like National Security Advisor Jake Sullivan and CIA Director William Burns—had ever dealt with before.

Abigail's kidnapping had other troubling characteristics too. Many of the freed ex-hostages displayed in Carstens's office, including Griner, had been prisoners of rival governments, a situation which could be dealt with on the basis of the hostage-taker's national interests. In contrast, the terrorists holding Abigail were foot soldiers in a demented ideological crusade. Hamas was not as accountable or pragmatic as, for example, the inevitably self-interested Russian regime that held Griner for over a year.

It was unclear exactly what incentives could move Hamas, but it was the job of Carstens and others in government to find out. The past offered a limited guide for how the efforts to free Abigail were likely to go. Early on, Carstens told me that this wasn't a sprint but a marathon. I did not like to hear these words. At the beginning I did not accept them. As the days passed, I realized he had prepared me for a harsh reality.

He also gave me one very important piece of information. While Carstens and his team took the lead in most hostage scenarios, the portfolio for the Hamas abductees was at the White House, with the president himself. Each day, President Biden received updates on the hostages in his briefing book on security. Abigail and the 245 people held along with her were a top priority at the highest possible levels of government. Knowing that Abigail's fate was on the president's desk every day gave me hope.

Carstens gave me his personal phone number and introduced me to Charlotte, a young deputy who would be on call whenever I needed her. Each American hostage family had their own version of Charlotte, a reliable and kind point of contact for the State Department's hostage affairs office.

Around the same time, I was also introduced to an FBI agent named Lisa, one of Roger and Charlotte's counterparts in intelligence and law enforcement. Part of Lisa's job is to travel to companies whose employees are at special risk of being kidnapped abroad—like big business, aid organizations, international banks, religious missionary groups—and brief their employees on basic hostage protocol. For instance, before leaving on a dangerous assignment, it is a good idea to make sure your bank accounts have another signer and that your taxes and estate are in order—you certainly do not want to be unnecessarily penalized for failing to pay taxes during your time as a hostage. Obviously this is not a top concern for three-year-old girls. But Lisa broadened my understanding of how US officials approach the special dilemmas of hostage-taking, and she gave me an acute sense of what a dark and complicated world the global kidnapping industry often is.

I was gratified to discover that US government officials really cared about our loved one. In every meeting, I sensed that if Abigail, God forbid, never left Gaza alive, these diplomats and investigators would feel that failure personally.

I was also struck by what Carstens didn't say in that first meeting. He did not promise to share intricate details of the negotiating process. I would not be getting daily updates on the government's efforts to free Abigail. As good as it felt to know that top-level attention was focused on the hostages, I left the meeting knowing as little about their circumstances and likely fate as I did when I walked in.

In this first meeting with a senior official of the executive branch, I realized that the men and women who implemented US foreign policy would tell you what they could tell you, but that they can't really tell you a lot. The government had negotiating strategies that it had to keep secret from its adversaries. An untimely leak could ruin a delicate diplomatic process, one that would come to involve at least four governments and a gang of off-the-grid terrorists dug in deep beneath an urban war zone. Next to such higher-level concerns, my own desire to free Abigail might not count for all that much.

I also learned what my role in freeing Abigail wouldn't be. I could tell Abigail's story until I was hoarse and build public awareness of her plight, but I was not a member of the negotiating team. I was not someone who could come up with new and creative ideas for freeing the hostages. I had to suppress a lifelong instinct to gain control over any given situation, the exact thing that had made me successful as a businesswoman and a community leader. I wasn't the quarterback. Instead, I was more like a ball, being lobbed between players that I couldn't always see, who were following game plans that were often a mystery to me.

***

It had been a hard week back in Israel. In Judaism you must bury a dead body as soon as possible. For the seven days after the burial, a bereaved family opens up their home to mourners, a ritual called shiva. It is meant to ensure that the bereaved are not alone, and that their community is caring for them during these difficult first days of mourning.

Kfar Aza remained dangerous for days after October 7, with Israeli security forces battling to take full control of the kibbutz and kill or capture every last infiltrator. Smadar and Roee could not be buried until October 18, eleven days after their murders. Like most of Kfar Aza, they were not religious people, but the Jewish state's inability to recover their bodies for over a week only compounded a sense that the state had betrayed its founding mission through its confused and pathetic response to the Hamas onslaught. Even in death, the government had failed my niece and her husband.

My daughter Noa attended Smadar and Roee's funeral in Israel, an event that was somehow both beautiful and unbearable. The night before, I texted my brother-in-law Dori and told him I'd be there in heart and in spirit. "Tomorrow will be a hard day," Dori replied. "But we will hug everyone here to make sure they feel loved [and] that they are safe." He was referring most of all to Michael and Amalia. "We will do everything possible to secure their future," he wrote.

Hours after the funeral, on one of the hardest days of her life, Shlomit received a call from Hillary Clinton. The former secretary of state offered her condolences and let my sister-in-law know that she had the entire family in mind. Clinton told no one about this and called at the exact moment when my family was most in need of a steady, sympathetic voice. No similarly prominent Israeli could match Clinton's decency—no one from the Israeli government called that morning, or in the days after.

Crowds of mourners descended on Dori and Karen's house during the shiva week. The surviving members of Kfar Aza—most of whom were living in hotel rooms, and none of whom had any idea when or if they would be able to return home—paid their respects, as did extended family, co-workers, and complete strangers. In a place as small as Israel, everyone knew someone who'd lost someone on October 7, or had lost someone themselves. Individually and nationally, the shiva process helped Israelis begin to try and process what had just happened.

Michael and Amalia never stopped being children as the mourners poured in, even with their parents and sister stolen from them in a single morning. They played with their three cousins, running around with the other children and keeping their spirits up, as if in conscious defiance of the sadness around them. Israelis were beginning to fight off their despair, no matter who they were. College students, high-tech executives, bartenders, and bus drivers dropped everything to join their reserve units on the borders with Gaza and Lebanon. Images of the hostages proliferated on stickers, posters, and billboards around the country, sending a message that the kidnapped couldn't be forgotten about or abandoned.

Abigail was just an hour's drive from where her parents were being buried. She was somewhere in Gaza City, inside one of the most fearsome terror fortresses ever built, a multilevel city of civilian decoys, disguised terror infrastructure, tunnels, bunkers, and missile factories. The Hamas terror state was defended using bombs and rockets hidden inside the above-ground layer of mosques, schools, and booby-trapped apartment buildings where the people of Gaza made their homes. At that early point in the war, the IDF was bombarding key Hamas targets like tunnels and command posts, most of which were located deep underground and could only be reached by dropping two-thousand-pound bombs near or on civilian structures, to visibly devastating effect.

Hostage families watched these developments with wariness. We had no idea if our loved ones were being held above or below ground. I had no idea whether Abigail was still with Hagar and her children. Perhaps the hostages were in a bunker with Yahya Sinwar and were being used as human shields to protect the Hamas leader from an Israeli strike. Later I'd learn that the IDF had bombed an area very close to where Abigail was being held. The building in which the terrorists had imprisoned her had been evacuated. The civilians fled following IDF warnings, but hostages like Abigail continued to be kept there under guard.

***

By the end of October, my schedule loosely resembled that of a member of Congress. I would spend weekends in New York or California. As soon as the work week began, I was back in Washington, facing a full slate of meetings nearly every day. I was committed to reaching as many leading figures on the Hill as I possibly could, no matter how divergent our views on other issues might be. Political differences paled before the imperative to save the life of a child.

In the first few days of November, I took an early-morning train to Washington to meet Steve Scalise, one of the most effective members of the ever-chaotic Republican congressional delegation. The Louisiana representative was in treatment for cancer. The meeting got off to a rocky start when he began to criticize the Biden administration on some minor point or another. But when we started talking about the plight of the hostages, the tension suddenly disappeared for good.

Scalise had a picture of his young children on his desk. His health scare must have been a difficult time for his family and for himself, but the urgency of the hostage crisis, and the fate of a kidnapped three-year-old, overrode whatever reasons he could have given for not being on the Hill to meet me that day. Regardless of any partisan differences between us, I felt nothing but gratitude toward him.

In general, my political views have much more in common with those of the left-wing "squad" of congressional Democrats like Summer Lee and Jamaal Bowman than they do with Steve Scalise's. Yet, while sitting with him, I wasn't so bothered that we didn't agree on reproductive rights or gun control. He cared deeply about Abigail's fate and was willing to do whatever he could to help out. I was grateful for this. If I could get along with Steve Scalise, anything was possible.

My meetings with leftist stalwarts were nervous, awkward affairs compared to my warm sit-down with one of the most successful and hardline Republicans in Congress. Representatives Lee and Bowman both listened to Abigail's story, and they even appeared to empathize to some extent. They put out tweets saying that they'd met with me. These were good meetings, or so I felt at the time.

I don't know how much of a positive effect they really had though. Lee called for a ceasefire just nine days after October 7, before any hostages were released—and with no regard for the fact that there *was* a ceasefire in place until October 6, which Hamas broke when it attacked Israel. Bowman was one of the most anti-Israel Democrats in Congress by the time he lost his primary in June of 2024. Clearly, to some, progressive ideology did not extend to the fate of a three-year-old Israeli-American child kidnapped by terrorists. How could this be?

The answer could be found in the dominant political binary deployed by the far left, which divided all of humanity into precisely two categories: oppressors and oppressed. According to this new political math, Hamas was not a gang of terrorists motivated by a medieval interpretation of Islam in which women and children were legitimate spoils of war; in which Jews and other non-Muslims had no right to sovereignty; and in which the LGBTQ, independent women, and other non-conformists forfeited their lives by failing to obey religious law. In fact, none of the group's actual beliefs or deeds appeared to matter one bit. Instead, these supposedly progressive members of Congress and the political faction they represent saw these violent theocrats through an ideological looking glass. They were now a legitimate national liberation movement fighting on behalf of "the oppressed." Nothing Hamas did or said could change that.

Jews, meanwhile, despite being one of the most historically oppressed groups of people on Earth, had become oppressors—a word that immediately licensed vile, age-old anti-Semitic tropes. Jews were now "white people"—a category that I had formerly understood to be the province of Nazis and other racists. Nazis never saw Jews as "white." Now a new kind of fashionable left-wing racism targeted Jews for being exactly what their greatest historical persecutors had slaughtered them en masse for *not* being. My own Iraqi-Jewish family had been chased out of an Arab country within living memory, and they were darker in skin tone than a lot of the Arabs in Gaza.

Abigail was beyond the sympathy of these progressive moral exemplars. She was not a three-year-old child whose parents had been horrifically murdered in front of her eyes. She was a white oppressor. The power of this twisted ideology can be measured in the numbers of educated people who ripped down posters with Abigail's face on them in every major Western city, including New York.

The message wasn't to abandon my old alignments or beliefs, though. I still believed in social justice, women's rights, and a host of other causes that I saw as connected to my hope for a better world in which more people could enjoy greater freedoms to love, live, and create things of value. What I understood now is that I couldn't simply use partisan labels as a guide to who actually shared my beliefs and goals, or to whom my friends would turn out to be. The needs of the post–October 7 moment had scrambled my usual political geography. What mattered now was reaching everyone I could with Abigail's story as quickly as possible.

***

In the first days of November, I had a breakthrough. Daniel Bleiberg, a college friend of my daughters who worked for Nevada Democratic senator Jacky Rosen, told me that a group of hostage families from Israel would be speaking in front of chiefs of staff and other senior aides to the members of the Senate Committee on Foreign Relations. The staffers are the people who do the real work on the Hill, and they can get a member of the Senate laser-focused on an issue they might not have paid much attention to. On November 6, the people who shaped the priorities and outlook of the legislative branch's foreign policy would be gathered in a single room, along with people whose sons, daughters, parents, brothers, sisters, and grandparents were in Hamas captivity—Israelis who were far more mystified about the workings of the US government than I was, but who were having fewer and fewer illusions about getting help from anywhere else.

Israel began its ground invasion of the Gaza Strip on October 27, which coincided with my birthday. It wasn't going to be a good day anyway, but this news made it a devastating one. The IDF didn't go in all at once but tested and flummoxed Hamas through a series of cross-border raids, which gradually snowballed into a major ground operation. Netanyahu's stated goal was to free the hostages and destroy Hamas—two objectives that were potentially at cross-purposes with one another. Israel's war of regime change in Gaza might make a hostage deal more likely, since Hamas could trade away the captives in an attempt to ensure their own survival. Or maybe the operation would make a hostage deal less likely, as Israel might come to prioritize Hamas's defeat over the safety of their own kidnapped citizens. The terrorists might also begin killing their captives in the hope that inflicting greater psychological horror on Israelis might cause them to crack, and cause the Israeli home front to crumble.

On the other hand, there were signs that Hamas wasn't completely irrational and was taking the threat of force or diplomatic isolation at least a little seriously. On October 20, the jihadists freed Natalie Raanan and her mother, Judith, Chicagoans with no Israeli citizenship kidnapped on October 7. The terrorists claimed this was a "humanitarian" decision, but it was possible they feared the consequences of holding American hostages. The Raanans' release showed that Hamas was willing to release hostages if the right kind of pressure was applied.

In the weeks after October 7, Israeli relatives of the kidnapped formed a group called the Hostages and Missing Families Forum, which held weekly rallies in the square in front of Tel Aviv's art museum, across the street from the Defense Ministry's headquarters. At first the Forum was not seen as a politically divisive group. In the early days, their rallies didn't attack Netanyahu or question the direction of the war. But the families themselves soon began to feel Netanyahu wasn't necessarily on their side, and that he actually viewed them with suspicion.

Part of this emerging divide was cultural. The kibbutzim in the Gaza envelope were mostly home to left-leaning Israelis, which meant that many of the hostage families were people who opposed Netanyahu's Likud party and saw the prime minister himself as an embodiment of political evil. On a more immediate level, the families were a constant reminder of the Netanyahu government's failure to protect its citizens.

Netanyahu made no real attempt to get the families of the kidnapped on his side. Instead, he treated them warily, and even seemed to see them as adversaries. While some members of the war cabinet held meetings with hostage families, the government did not assign representatives to each family or even reach out to them directly—Israeli families did not have a Charlotte or a Roger Carstens they could call twenty-four hours a day. They were seldom invited to private meetings with the prime minister or other top officials.

The Israelis who were experiencing the living hell of having a loved one held in a Hamas dungeon arrived in Washington in a state of unthinkable pain and desperation. Their attitude was: *Save us.* My heart broke for them. In three weeks of meeting with diplomats and members of Congress and appearing on CNN multiple times, I was beginning to accept that there wouldn't be an easy way out of this mess, and that a miraculous moment of redemption might not come. That didn't mean you didn't work for one anyway. These Israelis had to tell their stories just like I did to bring these staffers and their bosses into the growing army of storytellers who might somehow rescue our loved ones.

Many of the Israelis I met that day were survivors who witnessed the carnage in their communities firsthand. I had never actually met my young great-niece whose life I was fighting for. In contrast, the people speaking to the committee staff were fighting to free the people they were closest to. Each of their stories was horrendous and maddening.

The first person who spoke was a woman named Adi Marciano. Her daughter Noa was a nineteen-year-old soldier stationed at a base near the Gaza border. She was part of a unit of young women whose job was to monitor activity along the border with Gaza. More than one of these soldiers had figured out that something big was coming in the runup to October 7: they had seen militants approaching the fence with greater deliberation and less and less fear, and they had noticed suspicious movements of vehicles and fighting-age young men. Their superiors ignored each and every one of these warnings, some of which were given weeks before the attack.

In our meeting, Adi described what happened that morning with superhuman steadiness. The Hamas terrorists stormed the base while most of the soldiers were still asleep, killing many of them in their beds, women included. Noa and a number of other soldiers made it to the base's safe room, where she called

Adi. "There's been an attack. I'm in the safe room," Noa told her mother. "I just want you to know I'm okay."

Endless minutes went by after that brief call, which felt ominously rushed, as if her daughter wasn't fully convinced she was safe. When Adi called back, Noa answered and spoke only in a whisper. "I can't talk to you," she said in a disquieting hush. "We have to be silent, but I'm okay. Don't worry."

Noa hung up. By the end of the day, she was a hostage in Gaza. Adi began crying as she recalled that last conversation: "I never said I love you to my daughter," she told a stunned room of senior congressional aides.

I was the last person to speak. I realized I was the sole person in the group who held only American citizenship. The staffers didn't really know the story of Abigail and her family. But the first thing I did was turn away from my high-powered audience to look at the Israelis. "I was in Israel on October 7, but I got out," I told them. "My family was tortured and destroyed. But you live in Israel and face an even greater challenge. Seeing your bravery in coming to this country and telling your story is incredible." I turned to Adi Marciano. "Your daughter Noa might not have heard those words," I said, "but she knows you love her. Never doubt it. She knows."

Eight days after that meeting, Israeli forces found Noa Marciano's body in the Gaza Strip. She had been held near al-Shifa Hospital in the center of Gaza City. Israeli intelligence believes a doctor at al-Shifa, which was run by Gaza's Hamas-controlled health ministry, murdered Marciano inside one of the hospital's medical buildings. Even in moments where it felt like we were making progress, there was no way of knowing how much time we had left to save them.

***

That briefing for the Senate aides was held on November 6. The next day marked a month since the Hamas attack and the mass-kidnapping of the hostages. This grim anniversary meant another round of meetings on the Hill, for me and for the Israeli families. We met with leading Republicans, like Mitt Romney and Marco Rubio, along with left-wingers who are often skeptical of Israel, like Elizabeth Warren and Chris Murphy. We met Tammy Duckworth, a moderate Democratic senator, universally admired among Republicans, who understands the true meaning and horror of war like few elected officials ever have—she lost her legs in a helicopter crash while serving as an army officer in Iraq. Connecticut Democrat Richard Blumenthal told me that he had a photo of Abigail on his desk.

Our group for the day once again included people with unimaginable stories of suffering and survival. A young Californian had made it out of the massacre at the Nova music festival, the deadliest single incident on October 7, by hiding under a pile of bodies. These harrowing stories got the attention of even the most jaded listeners.

My role sharpened over the course of these meetings. I was always the closer, the final speaker who would clinch the group's moral and emotional hold over whichever representative or senator was listening to us. I would tell Abigail's story and then remind everyone of the purpose of our visit: to free the hostages—the women, children, young adults, and elderly whom Hamas was holding in defiance of every civilized rule and norm.

I was effective, in part, because I had become good at telling Abigail's story, which was especially moving and horrific.

But at least some of its power came from the fact that so many members of Congress already had some idea of who I was. The familiarity was sometimes cause for confusion. The night of November 7, nearly every member of Congress gathered on the steps of the Capitol for a vigil marking one month since the attacks. I stood next to Adam Schiff, the California congressman who became a national figure because of his crusading attempts to hold the Trump administration accountable for its many misdeeds. Schiff and I had known each other for ages, and my parents had been friends and supporters of Adam when he was a young leader in the California State Senate. Schiff was one of the lawmakers who personally called me in my hotel room the night of October 7 to check on me.

There was something surreal and nightmarish about being on the Capitol steps for a vanishingly rare show of bipartisanship in order to push for the release of hundreds of hostages, one of whom was my three-year-old great-niece. Uplifting as it was to see our lawmakers uniting in common humanity, it was all too horrible to accept. Among the members who didn't know me so well, I received looks that said: *What's she doing here?* They knew me as a Democratic activist, but they had only a vague idea of Abigail's story, or of how the slaughter of a month earlier had impacted my family.

The fact that I was on the steps at all, standing next to a prominent congressman during a major, nationally televised event urging the release of the hostages, did give me pause. Abigail, I realized, could become the poster child of a larger effort. She was an orphaned three-year-old—no decent person could possibly argue that anything justified her continued imprisonment. But there were 245 other Abigails, and every time I mentioned her, I also mentioned these other hostages, all of whom had stories just as important as hers. Every time I handed out Abigail's photo, I handed the poster with photos of the small faces of all the 246 hostages, making it clear these were real people whose lives hung in the balance.

Something could come of Abigail's plight: She'd help push the hostage issue into places and settings it might not have otherwise made it to. Even as she suffered in Gaza, she would help me make everyone care. Once they cared, the hostages might be freed.

***

By the second week of November, I had grown used to being exhausted. A month earlier, I'd sometimes let myself fantasize that the hostage crisis would be a passing episode, and that there would be a deal before the outbreak of all-out war. I still hoped for a deal every day, and, in a sense, I expected one. But I also knew better than to let each new day of Abigail's captivity send me into spirals of despair.

Time dragged on without a hostage deal, a daily torture of uncertainty. Within it were inexplicable moments when I got a morale boost, seemingly out of nowhere, when I needed it the most. One evening in early November, I got off the train after a week in D.C., more drained than I'd ever felt in my life. My phone rang: Vice President Kamala Harris was calling me. She and her husband Doug Emhoff had watched one of my interviews in their hotel room in London—the vice president said they had both cried hearing me tell Abigail's story. Harris had been my senator, and I knew her from her days in California politics. I was touched when I heard, a week earlier, that she and the second gentleman had met with some of the other American hostage families in D.C. She now reminded me, as a friend and a fellow woman, to take care of myself during these challenging days. It was a brief call, but it rescued me from despondency and energized me in the tough weeks ahead.

Every week Shlomit and I would speak. We would do our best to keep each other balanced and sane. At the end of every conversation, she would ask me if I was going to succeed in freeing Abigail. Yes, I would tell Shlomit—we're going to free her. I knew I had no idea exactly how this would happen, but Shlomit had suffered so much, and I had to offer her hope. And besides, I wouldn't have kept fighting every day if I thought I couldn't make a difference.

No amount of work, and no amount of hope, could banish the inevitable darker emotions, though. When I was back in New York, I would go for walks alone every night, wandering the empty streets by the Hudson River in the West Village and struggling to process everything. I would always walk past posters of the hostages. These fliers had become ubiquitous in parts of the city, which is home to the largest Jewish community outside of Israel. But since October 7, we were discovering that the city harbored its share of anti-Semites too—people who shut down highways, fought with cops, set off smoke bombs, and occupied university buildings, supposedly in the name of defending Palestine. Many of my neighborhood's hostage notices had been torn down and defaced.

I dreaded seeing Abigail's face attacked by the angry hands of people who might be my neighbors. As with that view of Ground Zero from my apartment window, my own local streets, a once-familiar environment, were becoming a source of disquiet. In a way, the sickness that had taken hold of these people's minds was as bad as the ideological virus that had infected the fanatics of Hamas. These were worldviews founded on resentment and hatred, which preached the destruction of the world as it is without being remotely capable of building anything in its place. I was horrified by this sickening convergence of radical hatreds in my own city.

The night walks often seemed like a metaphor for my own inner life—I was circling the neighborhood in the dark with little relief. At least I got to cry during the night, which was something I couldn't afford to do during daylight hours, when there was too much work to do. I would go home, get four or five hours of fitful sleep, and wake up the next day facing the same question as the morning before: *What can I do today to save Abigail?*

On some days, the answer was obvious. Early in November, for example, I got a text message from Ruby Chen, an Israeli-American, originally from Brooklyn, whose son was being held hostage in Gaza. Through him I was connected to a group of American citizens with family members who were Hamas hostages. Unlike me, they all held Israeli citizenship, and some of them did not live full time in the United States. They would turn out to form a new, albeit often dysfunctional, family, a family no one chose to join but one that would connect us all for the rest of our lives. We maintained a united front, keeping our disagreements mostly hidden from the high-level US officials with whom we met. We didn't opine on the ideal theoretical hostage deal, preferring to remain as apolitical as possible in the midst of a polarizing global crisis. We never leaked to reporters.

Of course, disagreements existed. These were people trapped in an incomprehensible hell, living through uncertain days and nights in which they were constantly imagining their children and parents being tortured and killed. But the group held together, in part because it was receiving professional guidance.

Through Ruby, and through subsequent conversations with the other American families, I learned that SKDK—one of Washington's leading political strategy and communications firms, was representing the Israeli-American hostage families in Washington. SKDK sometimes works with Republicans, but it is widely viewed as a Democratic shop. The advice they offered was effective precisely because it wasn't politically innocent.

There is something undeniably cynical about the families of Hamas hostages having to stake their success, and perhaps the lives of their loved ones, on whether they've selected a public relations firm that best suits the political balance of power in Washington. That's the world we're in, though: by virtue of its profile and access, SKDK can score meetings and media exposure on a level that vastly exceeds what even a well-connected activist like me can attain. Securing Abigail's freedom was part of a political game in which the hostages and their families were cards in someone else's hand.

***

Mid-November was our biggest chance to build momentum for a hostage deal. A number of leading American Jewish groups called for a rally on the National Mall, scheduled for November 14. The event, aimed at pushing for US support for Israel and the release of the hostages, was expected to be the largest primarily Jewish political gathering in American history. Congress and the White House would be paying attention. Rachel Goldberg-Polin, whose son Hersh was kidnapped at the Nova festival after a Hamas grenade blew off his left arm, gave an impassioned plea to the rally's three hundred thousand attendees, arguing that the world's moral conscience would be worthless, or totally lost, if it allowed her son to die in terrorist captivity.

In another speech, Orna Neutra, mother of twenty-two-year-old hostage Omer Neutra, talked about the events in her son's life that led up to him being kidnapped out of an IDF tank and whisked away to Gaza. Omer was a typical Long Island teen who loved sports—he excelled at basketball especially. He volunteered in Israel during a gap year before college and felt a powerful connection, which morphed into a sense of responsibility. The suburban jock decided to put off college and join the IDF instead. He became an idealist who felt he had no choice but to help protect the first Jewish country in over two thousand years.

These two mothers of hostages were the most affecting part of a long afternoon. Any woman at the rally could see themselves in these women, and likely asked themselves what they would do if they had to fight for a loved one's freedom from Hamas. Would they even be able to hold themselves together? This fight brought something superhuman out of people who had never dreamed of having to plead for their child's freedom with ambassadors and senators or of addressing a crowd of 290,000 people.

I was backstage at the rally with my daughter Noa, which was held on an eerily pleasant autumn day, with no sign of trouble from either the weather or pro-Hamas counter-protesters.

We met Natan Sharansky, the Russian-born mathematician and chess whizz who spent nearly a decade in a Soviet prison for daring to advocate for the right of the empire's Jews to emigrate to Israel. Sharansky went on to have an accomplished career in Israeli politics, serving as a Knesset member and as head of the Jewish Agency.

I had a picture of my parents with Sharansky at the December 6, 1987, rally for the freedom of Soviet Jews, which had drawn two hundred thousand people to the National Mall and helped make human rights one of the central issues of the late Cold War. It was painful to think that our roles were now reversed. At the first rally, it was my family that was trying to free dissidents through our activism for Soviet Jews. Today, it was Sharansky, appearing as a senior Israeli, who was here trying to help us. Sharansky knew who my mother was and said he appreciated her work advocating for his freedom.

The rally was a much-needed show of solidarity for an American Jewish community that felt more threatened and vulnerable than it had in many decades. Nevada senator Jacky Rosen and Oklahoma senator James Lankford, co-founders and co-chairs of the Senate Bipartisan Task Force for Combating Antisemitism, both spoke forcefully against hate. Rep. Ritchie Torres spoke of his support for the Jewish state's sovereignty, and Hakeem Jeffries echoed the support for the Jewish people and condemnation of terror.

The event's impact on the overall direction of the crisis in the Middle East was hard to gauge, though. Washington is a town where thirty people in a single room in a building no one's heard of can have more of an effect on the real world than three hundred thousand people on the National Mall. Because it's usually impossible to know which will matter more, you have to put yourself in every possible room, every chance you get.

The day before the rally, on November 13, I met a political operative whom Sophia Abram had introduced me to named Jay Footlik. Like SKDK, his existence exposes how American democracy often works in practice: to get results, you must work with people who know the system and who can represent your interests. That was true of hostage families, and also of hyper-wealthy foreign governments. Footlik was a registered lobbyist for the government of Qatar—a government which, in addition to other activities, had lavishly funded and backed Hamas, the terror group which had taken Abigail hostage and murdered her parents.

I now trust Footlik and count him as a close friend—if I were ever in jail in, say, Istanbul, Jay would be one of the first people I'd call for help. At first, I did not know what to make of him. The Qataris had originally hired him years earlier to improve their relations with major American municipal governments, and he had been involved in promoting the World Cup that the tiny Gulf emirate hosted in 2022. Footlik had been married to an Israeli and had in fact lived in Israel for a time, and he was the father of three daughters. He used to work for President Bill Clinton, and like Natan Sharansky he remembered my parents. Although my father had been dead for over twenty years, Footlik still had his phone number in the contacts on his iPhone.

Although I had come to trust Footlik personally, I still assumed that the Qataris wanted something from me. Qatar was one of Hamas's safe havens—Ismail Haniyeh and Khaled Meshaal, the terror group's most prominent political leaders, had lived in Doha for years, an arrangement that I understand the US and Israel supported from the start. Qatar was image-conscious, and perhaps sensitive to the impression that the October 7 plot had been hatched under the emir's nose. At the same time, the Qataris had become the Western world's preferred middleman in any big hostage negotiation in the Middle East, having helped facilitate several hostage-release deals between the US and Iran. The presence of Hamas leadership on their territory arguably gave the Qataris added leverage, and added urgency, in pushing for an agreement.

A lifetime in real estate, a decade living in Israel, and my growing involvement in the political world have all forced me to become a quick student of human nature. What is a person saying? Who are they? What's motivating them? I have the ability to know if somebody's full of shit, and I'm right about 95 percent of the time.

Footlik said the Qataris wanted to help and that it might be possible to meet their ambassador in Washington. I believed his concern was sincere and heartfelt. I told him I'd be willing to meet with his clients if they were willing to meet with me.

***

My next stop for the day was the Eisenhower Executive Office Building, the ornate, gray nineteenth-century White House annex that's home to the National Security Council. There, the other American hostage family members, along with me and Noa, would be in one of those Washington rooms of thirty people that could determine the outcome of major global events. We were about to have over an hour with National Security Advisor Jake Sullivan and his senior deputies.

I'd known of Sullivan from the hopeful days of Hillary Clinton's presidential campaign, although I had only met him in passing. If Clinton had won, Sullivan, then in his late thirties, would almost certainly have been nominated as secretary of state. Even at forty-seven, Sullivan still has the aura of a boy genius who reached the upper heights of government through his superior, world-shaping brilliance. I know that there's more to him than his cerebral public image. He doesn't smile a lot, but he'll flash a meaningful smirk when he's amused. While not a back-slapper or a particularly outgoing personality, he demonstrates a dry yet palpable sense of humor when the occasion calls for it. He is unfailingly polite, but never cold. In the days after October 7, he cried during a press conference as he discussed the sheer horror of the day's murder and kidnapping, something that complicated his otherwise-stony reputation.

Until that meeting on November 13, I had never seen Sullivan in his bureaucratic natural habitat, or even set foot in the Eisenhower Executive Office Building. In this new setting, there was something simultaneously familiar and foreign about Sullivan. I found him hard to read in the beginning—I could feel his intensity and sensed that he wouldn't let his guard down. As the meeting went on, I could tell that he had something he wanted to share but was weighing how best to do it, or whether it would be a good idea to do it at all.

Sullivan is very thin and often looks like he hasn't had time for a good meal recently, although it would be impossible to be one of the US government's most energetic foreign policy officials if that were true. In every meeting I've attended with Sullivan, he's brought in a cup of hot tea that he never actually drinks. He occasionally holds the cup, as an activity for his hands, or maybe an external source of warmth.

Sullivan's attitude in his meeting with the hostage families was guardedly optimistic. He alluded to the administration's exhaustive round-the-clock efforts towards a deal without going into any meaningful detail. Sometimes, he said, the difference between Israel and Hamas is like a square and a circle—the US and Israel, working through Qatari and Egyptian mediators, had to figure out whether it was possible to wedge these seemingly incompatible shapes into one another. In other meetings related to the hostage crisis, Sullivan quoted George Mitchell, the US envoy who negotiated the Good Friday Agreement, which ended the decades-long conflict in Northern Ireland: "You have one thousand days of failure until you have one day of success."

Sullivan knew a lot, but he also revealed almost no specifics, giving the accurate impression that he was one of the few people who was actually telling you the truth about the state of negotiations. In the course of advocating for Abigail's freedom, I discovered that you sometimes learned more from the answer you didn't get than from the one you did. Sometimes officials communicate through non-answers and trust that their listener will determine the shape of reality based on what they're refusing to tell them. We all left the meeting with an unmistakable impression that there had been very serious movement on a hostage deal. That meeting was the first time I sensed that Abigail could be on her way to freedom.

***

The Sullivan meeting and the rally on the National Mall were followed by a disillusioning meeting. Sullivan had shown real respect for the Israeli hostage families, and in doing so he became an avatar for high-quality American leadership. The sit-down with Biden's national security advisor was a conversation in which the few tense moments or bouts of real criticism ended in understanding. We were made to feel as if our presence was appreciated.

None of this could be said of the week's meeting with Israeli ambassador Michael Herzog, held at the Jewish state's embassy compound in a leafy residential neighborhood near Rock Creek Park, which I attended with my daughter Noa.

The meeting went poorly from the beginning. We met in a cramped conference room, a palpable tension in the air. A few days earlier, a meeting between hostage families and the war cabinet in Israel had ended in a chaotic and typically Israeli scene in which members of the public and their elected representatives yelled and screamed at each other. The proximate cause was that there weren't enough chairs for everyone, but the hostage families had deeper grievances, which the lack of seating neatly symbolized: they felt the government was both stringing them along and ignoring them, forcing them to beg for meetings. The debacle left many of the hostage families wondering whether Netanyahu and the rest of the government even cared about getting their loved ones back. Perhaps the prime minister saw the captives as an inconvenience and their families as irritating foot soldiers in a larger, decade-long conspiracy to humiliate him and end his career.

Ambassador Herzog is no Netanyahu loyalist. As a diplomat and former senior general, he has always been part of Israel's sensible, pro-peace center-left. But he is also a product of his own national and bureaucratic context. When the messy scene between government ministers and the hostage families came up, Herzog pretended not to know about it.

The meeting was conducted in Hebrew, a language in which I am nearly fluent. But I knew that you should never surrender any of your advantages in situations like this one and realized I had to stick to my strengths if I was going to give an ambassador a well-deserved dressing-down. "That is not okay," I said in English. "The people in this room are suffering. Their families have lost so much. You knew about that meeting. Everyone knows about that meeting. Even sitting here in America, I knew about that meeting." I noted that any hostage family member in the room could go on CNN, MSNBC, or Fox News tomorrow, or even later that evening, and talk about how shabbily the Israeli government had been treating them. They had so far declined to do this out of respect for the country and a conviction that they shouldn't criticize Israel too harshly in the midst of war. But the sense of doubt and betrayal was still there. Our loved ones were stuck in hell, and the Israeli leadership did not seem all that committed to their safe return.

"You'd better give these people some respect, because the only government that's looking out for them is America's," I said. "You are doing nothing for these people." Herzog had no real response. The meeting ended not long after that.

I had said what a number of other hostage families were also thinking. After the meeting, Adi Alexander, father of the nineteen-year-old American hostage Edan, from Tenafly, New Jersey, told me I was the group's "secret weapon," which I later realized was in reference to my leverage and freedom as someone who only had American citizenship. I was not Israeli, and I owed the Israeli government nothing. My voice carried real weight. But I got no pleasure out of saying what I had said to Herzog. On October 7, Israel had been caught off guard. Neither the state nor the society understood how much danger the country had really been in. The rupture of Israel's shared delusions gave way to a period of dazed denial. Even a month after the massacre, the country hadn't really found its footing. It was an ugly reality, and I hated seeing it in front of me.

It was true that Israelis had united like never before—that civil society had stepped in to give aid, basic services, and even military equipment that the government somehow lacked the capacity to provide. But the official confusion expressed itself through cruelties big and small, many of which probably weren't intentional. The coldness we received at the embassy wasn't a deliberate slight, but it was an expression of a terrifying sense of drift that Israel's government needed to reverse if it were to pull itself out of the dangerous morass in which a decade of wishful thinking and poor strategizing had landed it.

One way to reverse this drift would be with a tangible win. If living hostages were returned safe and sound to Israel, the government could begin to repair the damage caused by its complacency and incompetence. Abigail's freedom could be the beginning of Israel's comeback. Her fourth birthday was on November 24. I sometimes let myself imagine the party I'd throw her and the joy of seeing her alive and free, eating birthday cake and smiling.

4

One man held a veto over any hostage deal, and nobody knew where he was.

No hostages could be released without the approval of Yahya Sinwar, the sixty-one-year-old leader of Hamas in Gaza and the mastermind of the October 7 atrocity. Sinwar has a skeletal face marked with deep eye sockets. In photos, he gives the impression that he has never smiled once in his life. In mid-November of 2023, Sinwar was believed to be in a tunnel below Gaza City or Khan Younis, a miserable and dangerous environment that an ideologically craven militant like himself must have richly enjoyed.

During the first month of the invasion, Israeli forces began uncovering Hamas's sprawling underground city, a network of tunnels complete with command posts, dormitories, plumbing, electricity, food stocks, and ventilation. Many of the corridors were wide enough to drive a small car through. The Strip's three hundred miles of tunnels are one of the twenty-first century's most astounding construction projects, a logistical and engineering marvel built from smuggled materials and embezzled cash.

In times of relative peace, the tunnels ensured that regular Gazans would not have the concrete or money required to build much of anything. During a war, they ensured Hamas a safe haven while the people above them suffered and died. Average Gazans have struggled throughout the post–October 7 fighting, but there have been no photos of starving Hamas fighters anywhere in the media. In fact, there have barely been any photos of Hamas fighters, period. The tunnels are part of the reason why. They reflect the twisted values system of Hamas and its leader.

The tunnels to which Sinwar had retreated were the embodiment of his cynical vision. They also hinted at what he might be thinking in the midst of the Israeli bombardment. Sinwar does not care about the deaths of Palestinians; in fact, he uses them to help his cause. He thinks time is on his side—an extra day or two of fighting on the surface increases the global pressure on Israel to stop its campaign, while he remains safe and sound under the earth.

The sight of women and children dying crushes me, whether they're Israeli or Palestinian. But Sinwar has no detectable human feelings. A cold arithmetic has replaced whatever emotions he might have once had. Sinwar figures it will require massive numbers of dead for him to change history, and by late November the corpses weren't piled nearly high enough for him. The deaths that occurred during the extra days of the stalled hostage talks did not weigh on his conscience. Instead, they were a way for him to advance his grandiose strategy.

Sinwar is a known fanatic on the topic of hostages. He was reportedly furious when Hamas secured his own release in the 2011 trade for the kidnapped Israeli soldier Gilad Shalit, even though Sinwar had spent the previous twenty years in Israeli prison for strangling alleged Palestinian informants with his bare hands. Sinwar believed Shalit was worth more than the 1,027 terrorists Israel freed. A maximalist to the core, Sinwar thought Hamas should have demanded the release of all Palestinian prisoners and refused anything less.

Sinwar didn't stage his brutal assault on Israeli women, children, and communities on October 7 simply as a demonstration of Hamas's might. He didn't just do it for the GoPro videos or the notoriety. Sinwar appears to have really believed that he was going to destroy Israel. In the months after the attack, Israeli soldiers in Gaza discovered documents outlining Sinwar's plans for dividing the administration of formerly Israeli territory among his deputies after the war had been won. He imagined surges of Hamas fighters from Gaza, the West Bank, and Lebanon meeting somewhere outside Tel Aviv and destroying a military power that his fellow terrorist leader Hassan Nasrallah of Hezbollah has referred to as a "spider's web," a disgusting obstacle that can nevertheless be easily brushed away.

As confused and inept as Israel's military response proved to be in the hours after Hamas invaded, the country didn't collapse, even as fighters from Hamas's elite Nukhba Force made it as far north as the streets of Ashkelon. By the end of the day, Hamas had lost over one thousand of its best fighters and many had been pushed back into Gaza.

Sinwar was hardly deterred, though. His life's purpose is to wage war against the Jewish state with the maximum possible death count on both sides. He thinks of himself not as a mere general fighting battles in the real world but as a force of history engaged in a grand theological struggle. In his mind, even though his apocalyptic invasion plan had failed and Israel still remained a functioning modern state with a Western-level GDP, he had won a great victory by showing the Jewish state's naked vulnerability in a region where strength is the only form of political currency that matters. Every dead Israeli child, ruined home, and kidnapped civilian was another public wound to the heart of Israel's sense of its own viability and to its perceived strength. The more Israel suffered, the more Hamas gained, and the closer the jihadists got to some far-off, genocidal triumph.

How does a negotiator appeal to somebody who has no heart? How do you get to "yes" with someone who has nothing to lose, and who believes he's on his way to final victory, however long that victory might take?

During one of my meetings in Washington, I asked a senior Biden advisor whether Sinwar might be willing to accept exile and a guarantee of his personal safety as part of a hostage deal. I learned that the US government's read on Sinwar was that he didn't want to escape under any circumstances. He would stay in the tunnels until he died a martyr. Or else, he would emerge into daylight as the greatest hero in Palestinian—and perhaps modern Arab—history.

For the time being, this meant that any hostage deal had to follow a circuitous path. In Doha, Qatari negotiators would have to convince the Hamas political leadership, who were judged to be more rational if no less hostile and cynical than Sinwar, to accept Israel's demands, which themselves had been shaped by American and Qatari mediation. The Doha Hamasniks would then have to update their contacts in the Strip, who were now literally underground in the midst of a major war.

It was assumed that Sinwar had no physical contact with anyone who was carrying a cell phone, out of fear that the Israelis might be able to use it to track his position. The Gazan Hamas leaders would therefore relay their message by walkie-talkie to one of a handful of people who could meet Sinwar in person, or who could call into one of the tunnels' internal analog phone systems.

The go-between would then have to reemerge above ground before he could relay the terror leader's answer back to Doha. This process sometimes took several days. Sometimes it even took weeks.

Sinwar's lack of urgency stretched out the hostage talks. I sometimes thought that the Hamas leader must be exhilarated as Israeli bombs rained down on his people. The violence and chaos he'd unleashed was the realization of some of his darkest dreams. He had lived to see the fantasies he had nurtured through his lifetime of hatred and murder fulfilled on Earth, having dealt a worse blow to Israel than Nasser or Arafat or Hassan Nasrallah ever had. It felt to me as if he had sliced off one of Israel's legs on October 7. He didn't get the whole body, thank God. But I still imagined him shaking the severed limb every day, shouting at the Jewish state: *I got your leg.*

***

Roger Carstens and the rest of the senior US officials working towards freedom for Abigail always told me I would only know there was a hostage deal in place when a deal actually happened.

The media and the hostage families themselves were constantly being fed scraps of information by the press and others outside of government that weren't real, while the only people we had any access to who actually knew anything about the progress of the talks, the negotiating positions of the parties, and the actual prospects for success were American diplomats who were duty-bound not to say anything too detailed. All that Jake Sullivan or the people beneath him could say was that they were working round-the-clock to liberate our loved ones, even if we didn't really know what that meant in practice.

By mid-November, I had gained at least a schematic idea of what the efforts towards a deal consisted of. The mass kidnapping was unlike any other hostage crisis in history—there was no roadmap, no guide for what Israel, Hamas, the US, and other players were supposed to do or were likely to do. However, five weeks after October 7, there was a discernible tempo to the reported discussions and a semi-routinized channel for circulating proposals between the Israelis and Hamas.

The key to it all was Qatar, which is home to both Hamas's senior political leadership and the American Al Udeid Air Base, headquarters for United States Central Command in the Middle East. The hosts of the 2022 World Cup were highly image-conscious and therefore vulnerable to Western pressure. At the same time, as the hosts and financial backers of Al Jazeera, the Muslim Brotherhood–affiliated broadcaster, the Qataris were at least somewhat trusted by the hostage-takers themselves.

However one evaluated the Qataris' careful balancing act between the West and a murderous Muslim Brotherhood–affiliated terror army in Gaza, the country was in an ideal position to help ensure that Israel, the US, and Hamas kept talking to one another. And because of their involvement in the creation of the conditions that led to the October 7 slaughter—Qatar's hosting of the Hamas political leadership and its funneling of money to Hamas authorities in the Strip—the Qataris had a clear incentive to be helpful.

Yet the Qataris weren't involved in the hostage talks solely out of self-interest, as I learned on a November 15 visit to the Qatari embassy in Washington, a meeting that Jay Footlik organized. It turned out that Ambassador Meshal bin Hamad Al Thani had previously met with Hagar's husband, Avichai, who had been injured defending Kfar Aza on October 7 while his wife, three children, and Abigail were kidnapped. A diplomat from a country that does not think Israel has the right to exist takes on a real political and reputational risk by meeting with any Israeli for any reason. I am not an Israeli, but I am certain Al Thani knew I would be telling him a horrifying story about abuses committed by Hamas—a militant organization his country hosted for years.

Al Thani, a member of the Qatari royal family who has been the country's representative in Washington since 2016, wore an elegant Western suit. He was affable and well-spoken. Within a few minutes of sitting down with him, it was apparent he did not have any overriding political motives in mind in agreeing to meet with me. He actually wanted to know the stories of October 7—he grasped the massacre's barbarism and severity and did not think he needed to rationalize it.

The ambassador's basic outlook on the hostage crisis was markedly different from that of his Egyptian counterparts. While Cairo has better access to the Hamas military leadership in Gaza than the Qataris do and benefits from billions in American aid—far beyond anything Qatar receives—the Egyptians were not meeting with hostage families in order to understand their outlook and their pain. I tried many times to meet with the Egyptian ambassador or his colleagues in Washington. My request was rejected every time. Among Arab governments, the Qataris were rare in showing compassion for the victims of October 7 and their families.

We didn't get into any geopolitical matters during our meeting or debate the proper formula for prisoner exchanges or the broader Israeli-Palestinian conflict. We discussed the hostages as a purely humanitarian issue and as an abhorrent abuse of the basic rights and dignity of the captives. It was a conversation between two human beings.

Al Thani told me that he knew what it was like to have members of one's family held hostage. In December of 2015, gunmen from Kata'ib Hezbollah, an Iranian proxy militia, kidnapped twenty-eight people from a Qatari hunting party in a desert in southern Iraq, including several members of the Al Thani family. They were only released after a year and a half of negotiations, as part of a complex Qatari-brokered deal between Iran and Sunni jihadist groups. Qatar helped convince the terrorists to pull out of two Shiite villages in Syria; in return, Iran told its Iraqi proxy to free the Qatari prisoners. Hostage-taking has always been an instrument of state policy in the modern Middle East, and the hostages themselves are often small pieces of a much bigger game—except in the Al Thanis' case, the hostages were adult royals, rather than a powerless little girl.

Al Thani talked in surprisingly concrete terms about the actual Qatari role in the hostage talks. I had known Doha was the preferred venue for Israeli, American, and Hamas officials to discuss a possible agreement. Hamas and the Israelis were never in the same room together—the Qataris were both the hosts and the intermediaries, playing a similar role for Hamas as the US did for Israel.

Qatar's diplomats were a mutually trusted communication channel, conveying messages and searching for areas of possible agreement between two implacable enemies, but they also had enough experience in hostage negotiations to be able to raise new ideas of their own. They knew that a hostage deal required countless logistical intricacies, and that it would need to address seemingly small yet inevitably decisive questions of hostage transportation, monitoring, and second-by-second verification.

The creation of a brief window of good faith that could allow an exchange to proceed even amid a total absence of mutual trust and respect between Israel and Hamas was not something that could be taken for granted. It was an art that required skilled and experienced practitioners. If Abigail were to be freed, I understood that the Qatari diplomats would need to play an important role.

I left the embassy confident that Qatar had a heartfelt commitment to getting the hostages back, even if they were partly motivated by the need to clean up a mess they'd helped to create. But the fate of the hostages wouldn't be decided in Doha. It would be decided somewhere beneath the Gaza Strip, by a leader very different from Al Thani. And it would be determined, at least in part, by the ability of hostages' family members to pressure and convince our governments to act.

***

Since early November, when my daughter Noa arrived from Israel, we began working in tandem. We were nervous that, with Thanksgiving approaching, everyone would go on vacation—forgetting about the little girl, and so many others, languishing in Gaza. Together, and separately, we did press and Hill meetings every possible hour of the day. Our strategy was to talk about Abigail turning four on November 24 as often as we possibly could. Over less than a week, we discussed Abigail's birthday on-air with Gayle King, Katie Couric, and other leading television personalities.

I knew that our message was penetrating. President Biden noted Abigail's upcoming birthday in a November 13 speech. Bill Burns, director of the CIA and one of the US's chief negotiators in the Doha hostage talks, had also mentioned that Abigail was in danger of marking a birthday in terrorist captivity. Secretary of State Antony Blinken discussed the American soon-to-be-four-year-old hostage in a press conference after meeting with his counterpart in Israel.

The president and his staff hadn't gotten a call from me or anyone else in my family telling them about the upcoming milestone. They knew because we had been talking about it in the media and in meetings whenever we had the chance. I wanted to create an unofficial deadline: the world would have failed Abigail if she were to spend her birthday as a hostage.

I'd hoped all the talk of Abigail's birthday would also get through to the Israelis—to remind them that while the battle to win militarily against Hamas was important, it must not overtake the effort to get Abigail and the other hostages released. It was a dizzying challenge. Every single day my mind kept churning. *Why wasn't there a deal? What was I doing wrong? Who still had to be convinced?*

At night, my daughter Noa and I would work on putting together jigsaw puzzles to distract ourselves. But I couldn't focus on them, and it wasn't just because of fatigue. My mind surfaced the same awful thought, over and over again: *I'm failing Abigail.*

***

Then, on November 21, with just three days left until Abigail turned four, we got the sign we'd been waiting for. The Israeli security cabinet was meeting to consider a new proposal brokered in Doha. The cabinet's approval would be the last step towards confirming any hostage deal, and they wouldn't have been meeting if there weren't a deal on the table for them to approve.

I learned about the temporary ceasefire, announced on November 22, the same way the rest of the world did, through the news media. No one from the American or Israeli governments tipped off the families. This was for reasons of information security—if the terms of an agreement leaked too early, opponents of a deal within Israel or Hamas could maneuver to scuttle the accord before it could be implemented, or attempt to get a "better" deal once they learned what the other side was willing to give up.

The secrecy was also due to one of the unpleasant realities of hostage diplomacy. Nothing is decided for good until the hostage is physically present in friendly territory. Deals can fall apart at any time, for reasons no one can anticipate until they actually happen. Governments do not want to over-promise to hostage families, in part because the whole topic of hostages puts states in a netherworld of uncertainty, where their powers often suddenly prove meaningless.

The deal was straightforward enough. The guns would fall silent at 7 a.m. on November 24. Israel would cease all attacks but would not be obligated to withdraw any of its army from any part of Gaza. Hamas agreed not to launch rockets or so much as harass the IDF. For a period of four days, small groups of Israeli hostages would be freed through the Rafah crossing into Egypt. The exchange worked on a 1:3 ratio: in return for one hostage, Israel would free three low-value security detainees, most of whom were women and teenagers accused of various terrorist activities. If the first four days went according to plan, there would be another two days of releases, and perhaps even more after that.

The hostages that would be released over those four-to-six days would largely be limited to children, mothers, and the female elderly, excluding all others, even young civilian women. Hamas considered all other Israeli citizens it held to be soldiers, even if they weren't on active duty and even if they'd never served in the IDF.

It is a violation of logic and decency to consider someone a soldier when they are not in fact a soldier as a way of raising the price of their freedom. This logic, which Hamas dictated and which the various negotiating teams largely accepted, turns most of the Israeli civilian population into legitimate military targets. But there is much that is unjust about October 7 and its aftermath, and the conflict in the Middle East more generally. But we had to start somewhere. After seven weeks, Abigail could almost be free.

Or could she?

Watching the report of the hostage deal on CNN in my apartment, the doubts began almost immediately. Does Hamas know where all the hostages are? Can they even produce enough hostages to keep the deal going? Which hostages were even still alive after nearly two months of war? Was Abigail going to be released? Was she even alive? The family had received informal intelligence that she was, but nothing was ever confirmed.

The format of the deal gave Hamas plenty of opportunity for trickery. The two sides would have to produce a list of hostages and prisoners each day. Nothing was certain until Abigail was free. But we had reached a different, more hopeful phase of uncertainty, even if the next few days were among the most excruciating.

***

Noa, her boyfriend Yotam, and two of my younger children hunkered down with me in the apartment the evening of November 23. It was Thanksgiving, though it barely registered. It was as if the holiday had been canceled for us. We'd feel more like giving thanks—and eating—if and when Abigail was safe.

At that very moment, the hostages slated for release over the coming days had been moved to a central location where they could be easily retrieved, though we wouldn't learn that until later. Hamas was lying when it said that day that it still wasn't sure where all the hostages were. They were leaving the identities of the day's freed captives unknown until the last possible second, stalling and inflicting as much psychological pain on Israelis and Jews around the world as they possibly could.

By evening, the last second had arrived. A new gut-punch was coming. It was 11 p.m. in New York, and I could see the last few lights in the office towers of Jersey City reflecting off the still, black Hudson. The World Trade Center complex was nearly all dark. But it was dawn in Israel, the nervous final hours before the first hostage release, the largest and most complicated in the entire history of the Israeli-Palestinian conflict.

My phone rang. It was my brother-in-law Dori, calling from Israel.

"Abigail's not on the list," he said. "She isn't getting out today." Abigail would spend her fourth birthday as a hostage after all.

I had always assumed Abigail would be one of the first hostages out of Gaza. Perhaps there was an element of vanity here. By this point, I had made Abigail one of the most famous of the captives. The president, the CIA director, and the national security advisor all knew who she was and had discussed her situation in public. I had talked about her on national television over a dozen times. I had mentioned her to Hillary Clinton and Nancy Pelosi. That photo that I had given Susan Collins had become one of the icons of the post–October 7 period. For much of the world, a walnut-haired girl bursting with the special energy of early childhood had become the symbol of the hostage crisis, of everything Hamas was trying to destroy.

During my occasional lapses into fantasy, I imagined she'd leave Gaza on the shoulders of an IDF commando with a smile on her face and a krembo, the Israeli chocolate-covered cookie-and-marshmallow treat, in her hands.

On some level I knew my expectation of a storybook ending was absurd. But there had never been a hostage release like this before, and there were moments in mid-November when I'd tricked myself into believing in the inevitability of a clear, unambiguous triumph. But there wasn't one. I checked with my contacts in the US government. They had no idea why Abigail wasn't on the initial hostage list and what this meant for her safety.

On the night of November 24, my mind sank back into its now-familiar cycle of doubt. Perhaps I did something wrong? Maybe by making Abigail so well-known, I had raised the price of her freedom. Maybe through my advocacy, I had turned Abigail into an invaluable asset for Hamas's psychological warfare campaign. My mind seesawed between guilt and rationalization.

It was easier to berate myself than it was to imagine what Abigail must be going through in a terrorist dungeon—how terrified she must be, whether she was having nightmares about her father being murdered while she was in his arms, whether she took comfort from the thought that her siblings might be alive, whether she had enough to eat, whether her captors allowed her to use the bathroom. Was she still with Hagar? Did she know she had just turned four years old, and was she waiting for cake and presents for her birthday? Perhaps Abigail wasn't even thinking about any of that, and any happiness felt very distant.

It had been this way for nearly two months. When I left a meeting with an ambassador or a high official, I would wonder what it counted for if Abigail was still in captivity. As a family member of a hostage, you constantly have to see the possible sources of hope within the information you're given—otherwise the rest of reality would be too painful to face. You still have to sleep at night, which you can't do with your brain running in self-destructive circles. You take a pill in order to sleep four or five hours, before getting up the next morning to face it all again.

Tonight, the pills barely worked. Sleepless, I tried reminding myself of what I'd figured out weeks before: that in any hostage deal, there's nothing believable until the person is back in safety. We were still at Hamas's mercy, just like we'd been for seven awful weeks. The closest I could get to comfort was the thought that perhaps there was no deeper meaning to Abigail not being released on the first day.

And it was hard not to feel hope as I watched the twenty-four hostages who were on the list walk into freedom that day—including ten Thai nationals, one Filipino, and thirteen Israeli women and children, many of whom I didn't personally know but whose names and faces had become so familiar. Although Abigail wasn't among them, I couldn't help but feel joy and relief for these people and their families.

The morning of November 24 dawned over an eerily placid downtown New York skyline. Abigail's birthday was almost over in the Middle East. I sat with my phone in hand, waiting for any kind of news that would break the unbearable impasse. But none came.

I could not bear to call Leron or Shlomit and to feel their pain and disappointment. A few days earlier Leron told me that she had gone shopping to buy Abigail birthday presents. I thought of the presents sitting there, waiting for a little girl who still wasn't free.

***

The day dragged on in a haze of anxiety. No one had any idea of anything. Sophia Abram was in touch with members of Congress and was figuring out how to get celebrities to post pictures of the hostages on social media. Maybe more global visibility would help. Or maybe it would only raise their value to Hamas as bargaining chips. Maybe nothing helped.

I spoke at a rally outside of U.N. Secretary General Antonio Guterres's Manhattan home on Friday, November 24 to mark Abigail's fourth birthday. Back at home, the glare migrated across the glassy exteriors of lower Manhattan, and suddenly it was dark again. I no longer knew what to expect or believe. I felt nauseous. I could hardly bear to hear myself repeat versions of the same formulas I had learned to recite across media platforms and in closed meetings with diplomats and members of Congress. Despite my outward circumstances, I, too, was at the mercy of Hamas—living my life in a prison of anxiety, with my thoughts dictated by the deliberately unpredictable actions of my mental captors.

There were problems and delays on day two, with Hamas withholding the list of the day's releases until the final possible moment—a list that once again did not include Abigail. "No," was the simple text we got from Dori that night.

For a couple of hours, it actually looked like the entire ceasefire deal was off and that no one else was getting out. There was no promise Abigail would get out this round, or at all. Day two of the deal had gone far less smoothly than day one. I braced myself for whatever knife-twists were in store on day three.

Once again, there was no explanation on Saturday for why Abigail hadn't been freed. It began to feel like it was semi-miraculous that *anyone* had been freed, and after a second day of watching CNN, I began to feel guilty at my disappointment that Abigail wasn't out yet. Two dozen hostages were free now: I rejoiced in their freedom, but then the pit of doubt and dread would return. *Abigail wasn't safe yet. When would it happen?*

Then, around 7 p.m. on Saturday, November 25, I got a single-word text from Dori: "yesss."

***

It was 2 a.m. in Israel, but I called him immediately. Dori received the news we'd been waiting for, and I needed to hear his voice. The next day's hostage release list had been finalized, he said. Abigail was scheduled to leave the Gaza Strip that following afternoon, Israel time. Noa and I hugged and screamed.

We got ahold of ourselves again: we couldn't be totally sure of anything until she was back in Israel, something that wouldn't happen for at least another twelve hours.

We settled in for the third sleepless night in a row. We were either being set up for the most crushing possible disappointment, or we were on the cusp of seeing Abigail brought to safety. The next day would put us through the emotional wringer no matter what was to come.

The day's hostages were to be released at 7 p.m. local time in Israel, when it would already be pitch dark outside. In New York, it was noon, a gorgeous autumn day. Noa and I watched on CNN as a Red Cross van crept towards the Rafah crossing through a screaming crowd of Palestinians. Hamas had made a conscious decision not to adequately protect the vehicle carrying the hostages out of Gaza. The crowd, their angry eyes flashing beneath the television lights, shook the van as the hostages inside inched closer and closer to freedom. Nobody tried to stop the rioters. The result was to extract as much terror from the captives and their families as possible, milking misery out of every last second of captivity. Some of the hostages were forced to wave goodbye to the crowds, and to smile for the cameras, despite their terrified state.

At this point, we saw a grainy picture of what appeared to be Abigail's curls, in a ponytail, in the van. I thought of how scared she must be. Her last impression of Gaza would be the faces of an angry mob, and the fear of being bounced around by them.

Abigail wasn't free yet, I realized. It could all go wrong, in front of the entire world. Maybe that was Hamas's plan from the start. Perhaps the door of the van would open, and it would be empty.

There was a tense period where we heard nothing. Shlomit and Leron were on their way to the border to meet the Red Cross van allegedly carrying Abigail. The van was delayed, having to briefly divert from Rafah because one of the elderly hostages needed emergency medical care.

We watched on television as the van crossed into Israel and then began making its way, in the dark, to the Hatzerim Air Base, where Leron and Shlomit were waiting. Noa and I, in wordless suspense, stared at multiple screens—all playing the same scene.

Finally, we saw it.

Abigail in Leron's arms, being carried from the Red Cross van to a nearby helicopter.

Every helicopter carrying the freed hostages already had doctors onboard aimed at meeting the specific anticipated physical and psychological needs of the passengers. Because Israel is such a small country, some of these doctors personally knew the hostages they were taking care of.

Abigail, Leron, and Shlomit headed to the Schneider Children's Medical Center in Petah Tikva, a disorienting short flight from the place where Abigail had been a prisoner. She was much skinnier than she had been on October 7 and had lice in her now-short hair. She seemed distant and disoriented, uncharacteristically dazed.

The next morning, she was joined at the hospital by her brother Michael, her sister Amalia, and her cousins Inbar, Zohar, and Daniella. The moment she saw them, Abigail's face lit up.

***

At around 1 p.m. in New York, just as we were watching the van driving down that dark road, I got a call from an unknown number.

It was surreal to hear the calming lilt of the forty-sixth president of the United States on the other end of the line. "This is Joe Biden. I am calling to tell you that Abigail has just passed into Israeli territory," he said. "She is safe." No one announced the president or told me I was being patched through to a secure line. I was on a one-on-one call with the most powerful person on Earth. And I owed him a big thank-you.

I had met Biden once since his victory over Donald Trump in 2020, on a photo line with hundreds of other people. I did not want to blow my one opportunity to laud him for everything he had done for Abigail and the other hostages. A deal would never have happened without President Biden's leadership. Israel would have focused on its other war aims, and Hamas's high command would've been immovable and unreachable, if Biden and his team hadn't invested so much time and diplomatic capital in coaxing such utterly opposed parties towards a narrow and often elusive zone of agreement. The hostage deal was one of the unsung masterpieces of Biden's presidency, a reflection of the values of a leader who truly cared about what happened to the American hostages and to all of the hostages. He and his team saw the Hamas captives not as political bargaining chips but as people.

One of his great strengths as both a politician and a person is his deeply human ability to relate to other people's pain and suffering. It is all real to him. Biden might have unimaginable amounts of earthly power, but this hasn't made him any less interested or invested in human connection. I am certain he kept Abigail and the hostages in his thoughts.

In those few brief minutes that I had on the phone with the president, I expressed my and my family's gratitude for everything he had done. He listened graciously and shared his own happiness at Abigail's release, but he had to go soon: his next call was with Benjamin Netanyahu.

I was not the only member of my family the president had spoken to that day. Dori told me Biden had also called him in Israel as soon as Abigail was released.

I had calls of my own to make. I called Susan Collins and personally thanked her for being Abigail's voice and one of her biggest advocates in the Senate. Messages flooded in. "Hallelujah!" texted LA mayor Karen Bass. "Thank God...You willed this glory to happen," Nancy Pelosi wrote to me. "I cannot even imagine what she and your family have endured and am just in awe of the courage and absolute dedication Noa and you have shown throughout the last 51 days," messaged Daniel Bleiberg, Jacky Rosen's senior policy advisor. "We will not rest however, until all of the hostages are returned home."

A little after 5 p.m. New York time, Dori sent me the first picture of Abigail from the hospital. She wore a pink hat and was drawing a picture as Leron and Shlomit beamed nearby. *Had she been allowed to draw in Gaza?* I suddenly wondered. *What has this girl actually been through?*

In the picture Dori sent me, Abigail looked to me like the world's most beautiful four-year-old. She had lost her parents and her freedom and had made it back. While I knew that it would not be so simple, for a moment I let myself relax into the certainty that whatever had happened to her, Abigail was finally at least physically safe.

I then took my first real breath in months. The air no longer tasted sour. I exhaled. I could let go of a little of the anger, torment, anxiety, and panic that had governed my life since October 7. There was still so much to do, for Abigail and for the other hostages who remained behind in Gaza, but a significant part of my own broken world had just been repaired.

"I'm crying," I texted Dori, once I could focus my thoughts and emotions. "My heart is shining for Abigail. I'm so relieved she's safe with all of you. I know what a miracle this is in so many ways, and am cognizant of the sadness that her mom and dad are not there."

For the fourth night in a row, I tried to get to sleep without really succeeding. This time, the reasons were more positive. I kept seeing that photo of Abigail, a perfect little girl drawing pictures with her overjoyed grandmother and aunt. The photo was all over the news in Israel and the United States. Unless you'd been told already, you might never know it was a picture of a child hostage who had watched her parents die.

What else had she seen? I wondered. *What does she know, and how much of what happened to her does she truly understand?* These were questions for a psychologist who specializes in trauma and child development, and I was haunted by them even amid the rush of happiness. *She knows that her parents were murdered,* I thought. *She knows her parents weren't there at Schneider Hospital. What would their absence mean for the rest of Abigail's life, and for her ability to find happiness in the things that other children took pleasure in without effort?*

At least the idea of Abigail having a life wasn't a dream or an impossible goal anymore. She was safe and she was alive, I reminded myself—adjusting to this new reality. And if she'd spend much of the rest of her life coping with what she had seen and experienced, we'd make sure she would never have to do so alone.

Abigail, her father Roee, brother Michael, sister Amalia, and mother Smadar. (Photo courtesy of the Mor-Edan Family.)

Senator Susan Collins holds up Abigail's photo at a bipartisan Senate CODEL press conference in Israel. From the left: Senators Booker, Britt, Graham, Blumenthal, Collins, Cardin, Coons, and Tillis. October 22, 2023. (Photo courtesy of Hirsh Naftali.)

NBC's Lester Holt interviews the American hostage families. November 11, 2023. (Photo by Jade Klain.)

Liz and Noa Naftali at the March for Israel in Washington, D.C., wearing sweatshirts with Abigail's photo and the text: "BRING ABIGAIL HOME NOW." November 14th, 2023. (Photo courtesy of Hirsh Naftali.)

Liz and Noa Naftali on with Gayle King, *CBS Mornings*. November 22, 2024. (Photo courtesy of Hirsh Naftali.)

CNN's Dana Bash reporting Abigail's release. November 26, 2023. (Photo courtesy of Hirsh Naftali.)

The first photograph of Abigail free after fifty-one days as a hostage in Gaza, reuniting with her aunt Leron and her grandmother Shlomit. November 26, 2023. (Photo courtesy of the Mor-Edan Family.)

Abigail reunited with her grandfather Eitan, aunt Leron, uncle Zoli, and grandmother Shlomit at Schneider Hospital. November 27, 2023. (Photo courtesy of the Mor-Edan Family.)

Leron and Smadar Mor. 1990. (Photo courtesy of the Mor-Edan Family.)

Destroyed house on kibbutz Kfar Aza. December 6, 2023. (Photo courtesy of Hirsh Naftali.)

Liz at Abigail's home in Kibbutz Kfar Aza. December 6, 2023. (Photo by Alexi Rosenfeld.)

Abigail celebrates Hanukkah with her uncle Dori, brother Michael, cousins Inbar and Zohar, and aunt Leron just twelve days after being released from captivity in Gaza. December 8, 2023. (Photo courtesy of Hirsh Naftali.)

FOX's Brett Baier interviews the American hostage families. December 11, 2023. (Photo by Sarah Mucha.)

President Joe Biden and Secretary of State Antony Blinken meet with American hostage families in the White House. December 14, 2023. (Official White House Photo.)

Liz speaks outside the White House after the American hostage families met with President Joe Biden. December 14, 2023. (Photo by Jim Watson/Contributor via Getty Images)

Ofri, Avihai, Uriah, Hagar, and Yuval Brodutch. (Photo courtesy of the Brodutch Family.)

Abigail and Uriah Brodutch in nursery school before October 7, 2023. (Photo courtesy of the Mor-Edan Family.)

Liz with Adi Marciano, whose daughter Noa was taken on October 7 and murdered in captivity by Hamas, speaks at a Senate Foreign Relations Committee press conference hosted by Senator Cardin. January 17, 2024. (Photo by Brendan Smialwoski / Contributor via Getty Images.)

Liz speaking with Secretary of State Antony Blinken after the State of the Union. March 7, 2024. (Photo by Haley Stevens.)

CNN's Jake Tapper interviews the American hostage families. (Photo by Jade Klain.)

Liz speaks with Penny Nance, CEO of Concerned Women for America, to young female leaders. March 22, 2024. (Photo courtesy of Penny Nance.)

Secretary of State Hillary Clinton meeting with American hostage families. April 10, 2024. (Photo courtesy of Hirsh Naftali.)

Abigail and her family meeting with Secretary of State Hillary Clinton. April 30, 2024. (Photo courtesy of Hirsh Naftali.)

Abigail and President Joe Biden at the White House. April 24, 2024. (Official White House Photo.)

Artwork by Abigail presented to President Joe Biden at the White House. April 24, 2024. (Photo courtesy of Hirsh Naftali.)

Abigail under the Resolute Desk with President Joe Biden. April 24, 2024. (Official White House Photo.)

White House Coordinator for the Middle East and North Africa Brett McGurk pushing Abigail on the White House swing. April 24, 2024. (Official White House Photo.)

Liz, Abigail, and David Cotter with the Washington Monument in the background. (Photo courtesy of Hirsh Naftali.)

Liz speaking at Global Security Forum in Doha, Qatar with U.S. Special Envoy for Hostage Affairs Roger Carstens and NY Times reporter Adam Goldman. May 21, 2024. (Photo by Yael Alexander.)

President Joe Biden and Prime Minister Benjamin Netanyahu meet with the American hostage families at the White House. July 25, 2024. (Official White House Photo.)

Abigail and her beautiful family two weeks after she was released from Gaza. December 2023. (Photo by Keren Breen.)

Michael, Noa, Zohar, Zoli, Amalia, Leron, Daniella, Liz, Abigail, and Inbar.
(Photo courtesy of Hirsh Naftali.)

5

Abigail was free after fifty-one harrowing days as a prisoner of a genocidal jihadist group. Effective American global leadership, along with advocacy by myself and many others, had given her the rest of her life back. She would never be the child she had been before she was kidnapped and lost her parents. Her community lay in ruins. Her country was now fighting a brutal and often seemingly intractable war against her apocalyptic captors. She returned to a country and a life that could never go back to what it had been before.

Since October 7, the hostages were a microcosm for their battered homeland and people. If they were freed, there was hope that Israel could heal from the wounds Hamas had inflicted. If these 246 people of all ages and backgrounds had a future, Israel and the Jews had a future too. Their lives were in the balance, and their fate would be a verdict on what was in store for the rest of us.

But Abigail wasn't a metaphor or an abstraction. She was my great-niece. The people who were now hard at work giving her a solid foundation for the potentially difficult years ahead were people I had known and loved for most of my life. During her first week of freedom, I was texting them every day.

I badly wanted to be with my family in Israel but didn't want to visit too soon after Abigail's release. She stayed under observation at Schneider Children's Medical Center in Petah Tikva before moving in with Leron and Zoli at Dori's home. They were taking care of their own three children along with Abigail's siblings, Michael and Amalia. A family of five had become a family of eight, and its latest member was an orphaned four-year-old who had spent seven weeks as a hostage in a war zone. I wanted to keep a respectful distance until it made sense to visit.

That day came sooner than I thought it would. "I'm so happy she's home," Leron wrote to me a few days after Abigail was released from the hospital. "All we're waiting for now is for you to say you're coming."

Knowing I would finally get to see my family again, that these weeks of uncertainty had moved to a different and better phase and that I'd be able to hug and hold Abigail in the loving safety of our family, was as emotionally overwhelming as anything else I'd ever experienced. "Seeing Abigail back in Israel with you is a feeling I cannot express in words," I texted Leron after she told me I should book my ticket to Tel Aviv. "Abigail, Amalia, and Michael are so blessed to have you. I love you and cannot wait to come and hug you and Abigail and all the family."

"Harbeh a'hava," she replied—lots of love.

***

Having spent over a decade living in Israel, I understood the society's psychology enough to have boarded my El Al flight from New York with a real sense of concern. The Israeli national carrier was the only airline dependably flying to wartime Israel, but my own physical safety wasn't at the root of my worries. October 7 was the deadliest day in Israeli history, an attack worse in many ways than anything the country had endured. The massacre upended the country's entire image of itself—Israelis went from being powerful, secure, and settled to feeling weak, vulnerable, and confused. Hundreds of thousands of men between the ages of eighteen and fifty were suddenly thrown into a war that no one expected. Rocket sirens in Tel Aviv were a common occurrence, while a quarter-million Israelis from communities along the borders with Gaza and Lebanon had fled their homes, becoming internal refugees as rockets continued to rain down on their neighborhoods.

It is impossible to predict how such an unprecedented mass trauma affects any society until it actually happens. I prepared myself for the possibility that I'd be landing in a country I didn't recognize, a place where the shock and the pain were so immense and fresh that no one knew how to deal with them.

Somewhere over the Atlantic, I realized my fears about Israel were an extension of the same ones I had for Abigail and the rest of my family. No matter how hard they tried, Leron and Zoli couldn't set the clock back to October 6, and neither could anyone else. I wondered how much even the most righteous and caring and best-intentioned people on Earth could realistically do for children who had endured what Abigail, Amalia, and Michael had.

I was worried about what this trauma had done to all of them. If they could overcome the darkness, there was hope for all of Israel. But maybe the darkness was just too much for anyone. I was going to Israel to see Abigail for myself and to support our family. I realized I was about to begin the next round of my fight for Abigail's freedom, and that my opponents wouldn't be terrorists or a potentially indifferent public but something murkier and less tangible.

Pictures of the hostages greeted new arrivals at Ben Gurion Airport, hundreds of them lined up along the ramp leading to passport control. On the drive to the coastal city of Herzliya, near to where Leron, Zoli, and the children were now staying, billboards beamed the new wartime slogan of Israeli unity: "Yachad Nenatzeach"—together we will win.

What was winning, though? For some Israelis, winning meant the total destruction of Hamas. For others, it meant freeing the hostages. Togetherness was an unstable concept in an Israel that had been consumed by nationwide protests against the Netanyahu government's attempted judicial reforms the year before, and where there were such deep divisions.

As I drove up the coast, I listened to Kol Yisrael, the radio station, as it reported on the day's war casualties, the young men who had died fighting Hamas while my plane was somewhere over the ocean.

The sacrifices were steep—unbearable, even—but the Israeli people weren't shirking the biggest challenge in the country's history. Israeli flags were everywhere. No one was openly panicking. At the surface level, the society had indeed held together in the face of Hamas's brutal all-out attack, which was followed by a global campaign of isolation and defamation against the Jewish state by people who often claimed to want peace but who couldn't acknowledge the horrors Hamas had inflicted on Israeli women and children like Abigail. Israel had been put through the worst of national ordeals and survived. Perhaps it would even emerge stronger.

When I arrived at the house, it was obvious that my family had held up as well as possible. The challenges of the moment hadn't destroyed anyone yet. There were fifteen people in the house: the eight members of Leron and Zoli's family; Leron's parents, Shlomit and Eitan; as well as Dori, his wife Karen, and their three older kids.

The mood among the adults was somber. Their faces were often ashen as they hunkered down around a patio table drinking Coke Zero and espresso and smoking cigarettes. They talked about hostages, politics, and the war, the topics that dominated everything in Israel now. Abigail was freed on day three of the proposed exchange, but a few days later the deal broke down—leaving over 130 hostages still in Gaza.

Sitting with the family, I watched the children play with awe, thinking about how this little girl had been in a dark room with Hamas terrorists just weeks earlier. I admired how Leron's three older children looked out for and took care of the three younger children. I could see new relationships forming between everyone, ties that would hopefully prove to be sustaining. Watching them, I was reminded that as powerful as childhood traumas can be, resilience in children is nothing short of inspiring. At the house they were surrounded by their warm Israeli family, and it seemed to be what made these new circumstances bearable for Abigail, Amalia, and Michael.

It was the week of Hanukkah, a Jewish holiday that gave additional depth to what the entire society was going through. In the midst of Israel's latest war for survival, Jews around the world were celebrating the ancient Israelites winning their independence from the Seleucid Empire, the Greek power that had succeeded Alexander the Great's kingdom. After their victory over the neighboring Hellenistic king Antiochus IV, the Jews discovered a single bottle of ritual oil in the otherwise ruined Temple in Jerusalem. Miraculously, the oil burned for eight days, or so the legend has it—long enough for the Jews to reestablish the Temple prayers while waiting for new oil of acceptable purity to be produced.

The house was adorned for the holiday in decorations that now competed with banners reading "Happy Birthday" and "Welcome Home!" Every night we added a candle to the holiday menorah, to commemorate the miracle of that bottle of oil. This year, the ritual celebrated not just some long-ago triumph but the successful completion of another day—and the hope that we could all hold out long enough to become the bridge to a better future that our families and our people so badly needed. Visiting a bakery where we all decorated *sufganiyot*, the jelly-filled traditional Hanukkah donut, counted both as the day's main treat and as a little sign of healing. Abigail, her siblings', and her cousins' fingers and faces were covered in powder, frosting, and cream. It was a semblance of childhood normalcy for kids for whom nothing was now normal.

Back at the house, I loved watching the children play outside. Usually there was an informal soccer game, with Michael and his cousin Inbar leading the attack and Abigail, the smallest and fiercest player, hotly pursuing the ball wherever it went. I watched Amalia learn how to roller-skate. Inbar's twin brother, Zohar, shared his gem collection with me and told me where he got each shiny stone or crystal. Daniella, Leron's ten-year-old daughter, sat at the long dining table with colored pencils and produced amazing art for hours on end. Through all these wholesome scenes, I could not stop thinking about what all of these children had experienced on October 7 and what Abigail had likely been subjected to for fifty-one days as a hostage in Gaza.

Abigail was amazed one afternoon when I mentioned that I'd known her mother. *Yes*, I told Abigail. *I knew her when she was your age*. I told Abigail she was adorable and sweet—much like her.

I had to be careful with what I talked about around the three children. I couldn't ask them how school was going—they weren't in school. I couldn't talk too easily about family, since their parents were dead. Leron and Zoli were careful not to bring up Roee and Smadar too often, or to dwell unnecessarily on their murders. Like with any family tragedy involving young children, the adults walked a careful line between acknowledging normal grief, amplifying terrifying events, and constructing a façade of denial that suggested that bad things hadn't happened—the last of which could destroy the necessary refuge of a shared reality.

Abigail's time in captivity came up only once during the first few days of my visit. One night we were preparing for dinner at the house while I held my great-niece in my arms outside. Every moment I spent with Abigail amazed me—to see her alive and to actually hug this little person often felt as surreal as the fact of her having been kidnapped in the first place. We weren't far from Ben Gurion International Airport. A hulking passenger jet roared overhead, and I felt Abigail's body tense up. She clutched me tighter, as if she were remembering something that had scared her.

She had just spent weeks in a place where bombs fell from the sky, especially at night, and where strange, unidentifiable, relentless noises from the air were often the prelude to even louder sounds: the ear-piercing, earth-shaking sensation of a giant airborne bomb detonating. "Don't worry, Abigail," I stammered, doing my best to comfort her. "That's just an El Al plane full of people and children like you. It's going to New York, where I live." She softened her grip, and her body loosened.

It was the first sign that this child, who I'd just seen running around happily, carried within her a powerful trauma that few people would be able to see or understand, including me.

***

Dori was protective of access to the house. A number of high officials from the US government, including Jack Lew, the ambassador to Israel, wanted to pay non-public visits to the family. The answer was no. It was too early. While no one from Netanyahu's government offered to drop by and Israel kept up its official policy of chilly silence towards the family, they would have gotten the same answer Lew and his colleagues did in the first few weeks of Abigail's reentry.

The family needed time to establish some new sense of itself and what life together would be like. In fact, the family didn't intend to stay in Dori and Karen's house that much longer, despite the warm welcome. The effort of finding a new, more permanent house was becoming a critical part of the nascent healing process.

Only very close friends were allowed into Dori's house during these days. One of them was a woman whom I'd never met, but to whom Abigail owed her survival.

***

About a week into my stay, we were visited at the house by Hagar Brodutch, her husband Avichai, and their three children—ages four, eight, and ten. All three of her children had been in captivity with her, and since then her youngest, a boy, wouldn't leave her side. They were free now, but he needed connection and certainty.

I could also see the bond between Hagar and Abigail almost immediately. Hagar brought pencils and drawing paper. It turned out the art supplies fulfilled a promise she had made to my great-niece while they were hostages in Gaza together. When they ran out of paper and their captors wouldn't give them more, Hagar had said: "Don't worry, Abigail. When we're out of here, I'll bring you lots of paper and colored markers."

By then I knew Hagar had been with Abigail and her three children for every moment of their fifty-one days as hostages. She was one of those entirely normal people who, under circumstances none of us can really imagine—ones imposed without warning, which no one could possibly have been prepared to face—showed that she possessed superhuman reserves of courage, imagination, and love. A soft-spoken woman in her early forties, she worked in the Kfar Aza business office. She had lived in Kfar Aza for over a decade.

I could sense how fragile everything still was. I sat on the living room floor next to Hagar and the two four-year-olds who weeks before were competing for her care and attention in a dark room in Gaza. When we sat down to speak, I thanked Hagar for everything she had done for Abigail, but I was careful not to ask about her experiences in Gaza. It was evident how much pain she was still in. It would have been indecent to make her revisit the events of her captivity with her children, no matter how badly I wanted to understand what my great-niece had been through.

The few times she did talk about her time in Gaza, it was to reassure me about Abigail. "Of course I took care of her," Hagar said. "I loved her mom and her dad," she added sadly. She also said that no one in the group of five had been physically abused in Gaza.

When enough time had gone by, Hagar eventually did speak about how she had kept her three children, Abigail, and herself alive, including at a public event hosted by a Chabad house in Manhattan. "She's such a brave girl, and she's such a smart girl, and I have so many things to tell about her," she said of Abigail. "She's so precious, and she will be in my heart for the rest of my life."

Abigail survived because of Hagar's quick thinking, and because she had the continuity of a loving person who never let the four children in her care become demoralized. Hagar kept the children's spirits alive and kept them from losing their young minds or antagonizing their captors under conditions none of us can possibly imagine. At the same time, it was the task of providing for the kids' needs, and the mission of sustaining them through a nightmare, that kept Hagar herself motivated to survive.

Abigail and three other children have a future because of Hagar Brodutch's triumph over despair.

***

Based on what I learned in the coming months about exactly what happened in Kfar Aza on October 7 and in Gaza for the fifty-one days after that, Hagar fought a battle equal to anything the IDF accomplished, taking place on a front line that only a woman, four children, and a handful of terrorists ever had to see.

The night of October 6, Hagar's family had celebrated a milestone in any kid's life: It was her daughter Ofri's tenth birthday. She had reached double digits. Grandparents, uncles, and cousins gathered in their one-story house in Kfar Aza. Hagar and Avichai had moved to the kibbutz a decade earlier and thought of it as paradise on Earth, a place where children could run around without their parents having to worry about them.

That Friday night, after the party, Hagar put her three children to bed. A couple of miles to the west, Hamas commandos were already getting into position for the next morning's rampage.

Word of an infiltration reached Avichai just before 6:30 a.m. An estimated three hundred terrorists were in Kfar Aza throughout October 7, but in the early hours it was impossible for anyone to know the scope of the emergency. The family had felt safe in the kibbutz—the houses were equipped with shelters, the IDF was nearby, the kindergarten had walls of reinforced concrete, and direct rocket strikes were rare enough that the bolder and more curious kibbutzniks would sometimes go outside to watch the defense system intercept the incoming missiles.

Avichai was one of the community's fourteen volunteer security officers. That morning, he sensed that the situation was serious enough to justify putting on his IDF reservist uniform—that way other members of the Kfar Aza security team, and, if needed, Israeli police and military, would be able to tell him apart from infiltrators, in theory. One thing he didn't have was his M16 rifle. A year earlier, after a superficially impressive Israeli bombing campaign seemed to have solved all Gaza-related security issues, the government had advised Avichai and his colleagues that they no longer needed to keep their guns at home. The weapons were now stored in a centrally located armory that Avichai needed to get to as quickly as possible. He barely had time to hug Hagar and assure her he'd be back soon.

When he opened the door to leave, he saw a terror-flushed three-year-old soaked in blood. She had come there intentionally. Avichai and Hagar's four-year-old son, Uriah, was her friend, and their parents were close. In the midst of unimaginable panic, this capable three-year-old navigated a war zone to get herself to a friend's house. And yet, when she saw Avichai, she at first turned around to run away—behavior that puzzled Avichai, whose knowledge of the emergency paled in comparison to Abigail's. Abigail had just watched Hamas terrorists, disguised in convincing fake IDF uniforms, murder her parents.

When he caught her, he was both relieved and unsettled to discover the blood wasn't hers. He put her in the safe room with his wife and children and left to defend his home.

In the safe room, Abigail was relieved to see Uriah. Abigail told them she'd watched terrorists kill her parents. She had been in her father's arms when he'd been shot, crawled out from under his dead body, and ran to the house of her family's close friends, Hagar and Avichai. Perhaps Abigail had one of those preternatural childhood instincts that Hagar was the right person to protect her.

As Hagar struggled to understand the situation beyond their "safe room," she tried to remain calm for the children. Clearly something very serious was happening. Avichai wasn't back yet. But there was reassurance to be found in the severity of what was going on out there: if the situation was truly dangerous, then the IDF would surely be there soon, and they would all be rescued. Armed with that conviction, they spent the next four hours in the safe room, which Hagar left once to retrieve snacks and a change of clothes for Abigail.

In reality, safety was a long way off. Avichai was in the minority of security officers who made it to the armory alive. He watched his friends die right next to him as they sprinted to the one-room concrete shack at the edge of the kibbutz's central green.

Once the surviving volunteers had retrieved their M16s, they discovered that the terrorists, who outnumbered them badly, were avoiding gunfights. Hamas's elite soldiers were much more interested in killing and kidnapping unarmed people than they were in proving their courage in battle. In cases when the terrorists decided a fight was unavoidable, the Kfar Aza fighters were outgunned. Avichai endured a storm of grenades and RPG fire.

He was injured in his leg and arm, and a friend had to drag him to safety. He was helicoptered out of the kibbutz and to a nearby hospital at 2 p.m., seven and a half hours after he'd locked his family in the safe room where they were presumably still hiding.

In another area of the kibbutz, it would be seven more hours before Israeli security forces extracted Michael and Amalia from their closet. From there, the children were taken by rescuers to the home of an aunt and uncle.

It would take twenty-two more hours for Leron, Zoli, and their three kids, along with a neighbor and her one-month-old baby, to be rescued from where they were, barricaded together behind a reinforced safe-room door. They heard Hamas terrorists all around their home and listened to hours of gunshots and grenade explosions. They heard terrorists in their own house a few feet away from where they hid in silence, desperately hoping they would not be discovered.

Once rescued by the IDF, they left Kfar Aza in two vehicles of an army convoy: Leron, Daniella, and Zohar in one; Zoli and Inbar in the second. On the road north, Zoli saw the aftermath of both a day of unthinkable security failures and of a much longer period of large-scale strategic and societal delusion. Everywhere he looked on the two-lane road connecting the southern kibbutzim to the highway, there were burned-out cars and dead bodies. Zoli made Inbar put his head down. He didn't want someone so young whom he loved so much to see so much destruction.

***

At around 11 a.m., fifteen terrorists dressed in balaclavas and olive military gear arrived at Hagar's door. The slaughter at Kfar Aza, which would leave sixty-three of the town's eight hundred residents dead and another eleven in Hamas captivity, had been going on for over four and a half hours. The terrorists still had free reign over the border town. After entering her home, they forced open the safe room with relative ease. There, they discovered a four-year-old boy, an eight-year-old boy, and a ten-year-old girl, along with a woman in her early forties.

Hagar noticed that Abigail was hiding under a pile of blankets. In the confusion, it occurred to her that it might be possible to keep the three-year-old hidden while the rest of them were taken away, presumably as hostages. Then she realized there was no guarantee Abigail would be any more protected if she were left alone in the abandoned house, with Hamas fighters going door to door, than she would be as a hostage. At least in the latter instance, there was a chance Hagar could try to protect the child. She helped Abigail put on a pair of Uriah's shoes. She would take Abigail with her as one of her own children.

Everyone stayed remarkably calm in the moment, although perhaps the shock of being taken from their home by men with guns overwhelmed any stabs of panic. The terrorists told Hagar to bring them her car keys.

There is no road connecting Kfar Aza, which is Hebrew for "Gaza village," to the kibbutz's namesake city, which is less than one mile away. Ever since the 2005 withdrawal of Israeli forces from Gaza and Hamas's 2007 takeover of the coastal enclave, the fence behind the kibbutz has been a border with a hostile neighboring population, even if twenty thousand Gazans still had permits to work inside of Israel—some of them at Kfar Aza. To get back to Gaza, the Hamas terrorists had to race across the fields in Hagar's compact car in order to reach the gap they'd blasted into the security fence, a billion-dollar undertaking that provided no real security at the moment it was most needed.

Once in Gaza, Hagar's car, crammed with four children, one woman, and two terrorists, jolted down rough fields, past the jumble of flimsy concrete cubes that layered the low hills across from the kibbutz. As they drove off, Hagar experienced the disembodied feeling of being on the other side of an uncrossable line, in a place she never was supposed to be in for any reason. In addition to her own life, she was responsible for the lives of four children in this place, a foreign and forbiddingly hostile environment.

It soon became clear that Hagar and the children had arrived on the happiest day in that place's sad recent history. The people were overjoyed because of her—in a way, the noxious party Hagar saw in the streets was being thrown for her and the children. Crowds swelled around an impromptu parade of triumphant Hamas warriors as the five captives crept past the high-rises of central Gaza City. The Gazans cheered, chanted, and screamed in glee, celebrating the only real victory over the Israeli enemy that they'd ever gotten to see in their lives. Hagar and the young captives were the substance and proof of that success.

One of the terrorists struck Hagar and pulled her by the hair as the crowd looked on, the only time she'd be beaten across fifty-one days in captivity. He then grabbed Ofri, the girl who had just turned ten years old, and shoved her upper body out of the window of the cramped car. A great cheer went up from the intoxicated masses of Gazans at seeing this reward. Here was the return on their support for Hamas; for the bombed-out and rocketed buildings where families lived and which were also used by fighters; for fields that were turned into launching pads; for necessities like concrete that were diverted to building networks of underground tunnels; for the transformation of schools into factories for young martyrs; for the taxes the jihadists levied on bread, rice, lentils, and sweets so that Hamas could buy weapons and build rockets for its army of terror.

Here was the defeated enemy, in the form of a captive and petrified ten-year-old girl.

***

There is no Kfar Aza anymore, the terrorists told Hagar. There is no Israel. Your community and your country are gone. In the grip of her own fear and terror, with no doubt as to her captors' capacity for cruelty and under conditions of total dependence for food and water, requiring permission to go to the bathroom, Hagar believed them. Mental adaptation to a hostage-taker's lies is a phenomenon that psychiatrists who have studied kidnapping say is normal. In some cases, it can be life-saving.

In a strange way, Hagar and the children survived because she believed her captors about the destruction of her old life. There was no kibbutz left, maybe no country left—nothing to return to. She assumed her husband was dead, though she tried not to think about it and fall into debilitating grief. All Hagar had left was these four children. Her world now consisted entirely of them, and she would pour all of her energy and creativity into ensuring their physical and mental survival and into maintaining a small ray of hope that their nightmare might somehow end.

At first they were held in the top-floor unit of a low-rise apartment building in a small room. The windows were completely covered. During the day they could see some light peeking in. The nights were pitch black. They were in the dark.

The apartment belonged to a reasonably well-off Gazan family who served as the hostages' co-jailors. The husband revealed to Hagar in one of the brief conversations at the beginning of their stay that he was a member of Hamas. They had children of their own, including a young child named Ahmed.

A young woman named Emily from Kfar Aza, whose fingers had been blown off in the attack, was being held there along with them. During the day, Fatima, the wife of the main Hamas captor, made sure the six captives were fed on a just-better-than-starvation diet of instant noodles, pita bread, and hummus. The bathroom had no running water, and Hagar often had to ask for toilet paper on the group's behalf. They were given three toothbrushes for the six of them.

Hagar was always careful not to speak to any of her jailers more than was necessary. She did not want to accidentally say anything that could give the hostage-takers more of an advantage than they already enjoyed. She accepted that she had no choice but to keep four children entertained in a dark room for what could be weeks or months or even years. So she bargained carefully with the terrorists for paper, pencils, and a few decks of playing cards. Emily was a source of comfort, especially for Ofri.

The games they played were quiet. They couldn't make any noise—the terrorists worried that someone might hear Hebrew being spoken and betray the hostages' location to the Israelis. Hagar had to keep the kids from speaking loudly or generally behaving the way children normally would. She taught her two older kids to play solitaire, which meant they could keep themselves busy in times when she had to attend to one of the other young kids' needs. During the long days, the younger kids at times could keep themselves occupied with pencil and paper. All of them needed Hagar's attention, and they all had to wait their turn.

There was one teasing false dawn about a week and a half into captivity when Hagar let herself believe that freedom might be near. The captor's wife announced that they were going to buy the hostages new clothes. Hagar thought this meant they would all be released soon—after all, the hostages had to look fresh and well cared for in order for Hamas to reap its requisite propaganda victory for letting the Israeli children leave Gaza alive.

But things only got worse from there. Bombs rained down and no one was released. Abigail was thrilled for a moment about her new clothes, though. In the midst of all the horror, she retained a three-year-old's joy at getting presents, in this case a badly needed change of clothes.

***

The bombing was worse at night, and Hagar was thankful that the children could fall asleep while deadly thunderclaps got closer and closer. On some nights, Hagar could hear the sounds of machine guns and rocket fire. She rarely slept. She stayed up worrying whether they'd all survive the next day or whether they'd die along with their captors.

In the mornings, Abigail often woke up complaining of stomachaches. She, like the other children and Hagar, was starving. But Hagar knew this was also a three-year-old's expression of anxiety and despair. The aches were the main overt manifestation of the deep sadness within Abigail. She did not panic or cry that much, though. *This is a resilient little girl*, Hagar thought to herself. She spent hours just holding Abigail, trying to keep the both of them steadied.

One night, almost two weeks after the kidnapping, the bombs finally made it to their block. The buildings in Gaza are made out of cheap concrete because for years Hamas has diverted the best building materials into the underground city it has constructed for its fighters. A neighboring building went down in a black cloud of fire and ash. A chunk of the building slammed into the side of the apartment. Debris struck Ofri in her hand and head.

Hagar had just watched her ten-year-old daughter sustain a war injury. Israeli parents live with the knowledge that their children, most of whom go on to serve in the army when they reach the age of eighteen, might one day be wounded or killed in war. But ten seemed a grotesquely early age at which to see this fear realized. Her daughter now needed medical attention in a conflict zone in which the hospitals were being used as terrorist command posts.

Hagar and the four children were driven in an ambulance to a hospital parking lot. A paramedic came out to meet them and cleaned up Ofri's wounds, which were deep enough to leave a scar on one hand. Ofri did not cry or scream—she remained stoically calm, as if she'd learned in recent weeks that war and its horrors were now an intimate and sadly unremarkable aspect of life. The guards let the children run into the hospital to use the bathroom. Hagar's heart dropped watching them go; she held her breath until they returned. It was the only time she had been separated from the children.

From the parking lot, they were then taken to another location, in a less threatened section of Hamas's besieged and rapidly shrinking domain. Emily did not go with them to the new house.

***

Their next prison was the abandoned home of a wealthy Palestinian family, now wasted as a terrorist gang's prison for hostages. It was squalid. Hagar and the four children were put in the room of the absent family's three-year-old child. None of the children felt comfortable sleeping on the bed of the small child whose room they were staying in, so they all slept together on the floor.

Some nights the bombing was so close and intense that they were moved to a small room in a lower apartment. Even on these nights, after the two little children fell asleep, Hagar spent hours talking to her two older children about what they would do when they went back to Israel, making sure that they stayed hopeful in spite of her own personal doubts.

Hagar and the four children were under the constant watch of three Hamas guards, experienced militants in their twenties and thirties, as well as their somewhat older commander, a harsh man who denied basic necessities to the hostages, perhaps in the hopes that Hagar would beg him for them. Hagar and her captors spoke enough English between them to communicate. She had to ask for toilet paper and cleaning supplies. She needed soap to clean the bathroom and the children. The commander savored every "no."

Even casual cruelty has limits. Not all human beings share a taste for humiliating and torturing others, even if they are on opposite sides in a war. The commander's subordinates were not especially nasty and eventually granted requests for toilet paper and soap. Hagar asked for extra food for the children as their meals dwindled to almost nothing. This request was almost always denied. She often split her own daily piece of pita among her four charges.

One day the commander left and never returned. Hagar lacked any sure knowledge about anything beyond the four walls of their prison. The guards would let the children watch Arabic-dubbed cartoons some afternoons, but they never accidentally flipped to a news channel or to anything that might allow their captives a window into outside events. Hagar didn't know that the IDF had invaded Gaza and was chasing Hamas south from Gaza City. She didn't know that her husband, Avichai, was not only alive, but had camped out in front of the Defense Ministry headquarters in Tel Aviv and refused to leave, and he had traveled across Europe and to the United States to plead for his family's freedom.

Hagar filled the time by inventing memory games. She would challenge the kids to list all of their relatives, all the aunts and uncles and cousins they could think of, and then describe how they were related to each one. Instead of receiving food to eat, they played a game of what meal they would each eat once they were back in Israel.

Hagar did her best to balance her attention between the four children, who became agitated if they were ignored for too long. The children didn't always get along with each other. They were different ages and sick of being together with so little to do. Of course, young children don't get along even when they aren't hostages, and they get bored even when there is no shortage of possibilities for distraction.

The smallest stimuli became psychic enormities. The guards made tea every day. The smell of it brewing became like torture to Hagar. She grew desperate for more food and for anything that might distract the children and somehow add to their chances for survival. But she never asked for tea.

Hagar wore a necklace that the terrorists had never gotten around to seizing. Maybe I should give one of the guards my necklace, Hagar suggested to Ofri, in exchange for more food. Ofri, the ten-year-old girl who had been held out the window to the screaming crowd and injured in an airstrike, was the voice of rational distrust: if you give the necklace to them, she said, they may take it and not give us the food.

In this moment, it really sank in to Hagar: *If we remain hostages, we might starve or die from the bombs. If we live, I'll be bringing my children back to a destroyed home without their father, to a ruined country, a life erased from existence.*

***

Toward the end of November, hope waned, food nearly vanished, and monotony set in. The streets outside the house that had been eerily silent in between bombing started to fill with the sounds of people and animals returning to the neighborhood. The loud bombing stopped. Word came that the five were being moved again. Hagar had been keeping track of the time closely enough to know that one of the next days was Abigail's birthday. She did not know it would also be the first day of the eventual six-day ceasefire between Israel and Hamas, in which scores of hostages would be released.

They were transported to a new location. Hagar wore a hijab, and the kids were forced to keep their heads down and not look out the windows. At this new and final way station, one of the guards told Hagar that she and the children were about to be freed. When she told another guard that it was Abigail's fourth birthday, he brought some candy. When Abigail ate it, she got an awful stomachache—after seven weeks near starvation, even a few pieces of candy were more than her digestive system could handle.

When Hagar and the children left their last prison, and she was able to see the children in full daylight for the first time since October 7, she noticed how dirty and discolored the children's skin and hair were. She saw how much weight they'd lost and how unhealthy they all looked. She was amazed at the deprivation the darkness and fear had hidden from her, and from them.

Maybe the rest of life would also be like that, she thought. Maybe they'd keep discovering new layers of horror to their experience and things they'd blocked out. But they were alive. Whatever had happened to them, and whatever was still waiting for them, they were all alive.

Nearly two months earlier, Hagar and the children became trophies of war, proof that Israel and the Jewish people had been defeated and that Hamas had fulfilled its darkest dreams. In freedom, the ex-hostages could demonstrate the opposite possibility—that there was a future life beyond the horrors they had endured. Within the darkness, they were the stubborn and sustaining glimmers of light.

6

I spent the first week of December at the house with my family in Israel. I wanted to spend every possible moment with Leron and the kids. Aside from attending the weekly Saturday night rally to push for a renewed hostage deal, I didn't even go to Tel Aviv, just thirty minutes away. Everything that had happened since October 7 made our time together precious. For my own peace of mind, I needed to go back to the US confident that Abigail's captivity hadn't gutted her capacity for happiness, and that the family had a path to a new future.

There were some things I didn't want to see. I had turned down multiple offers to see the Israeli government's forty-seven-minute reel of footage of the October 7 attack, which was so disturbingly violent that it could only be viewed by invitation. My friend Penny Nance saw the film not long after the attack, and I took her advice not to see it. "I'll have borne witness for you," Nance offered.

In December I could see the wreckage of October 7 continue to play out every day in Israel. In a way, I was part of that wreckage. I didn't need any additional help visualizing Smadar and Roee's murders because I had replayed them in my mind so many times.

But I had to see Kfar Aza. I felt there were things about the past two months, and about my family, that I could never fully understand unless I went to the site of the murders and kidnappings that had consumed so much of my life, events that now also defined the larger, suddenly more tenuous existence of Jewish people and Israel.

Although it was only ninety minutes to the south, a day trip from Karen and Dori's house would not be easy: Hamas was firing mortars and rockets over the border nearly every single day, mostly hitting empty buildings in towns that had been evacuated almost two months earlier. The road to Kfar Aza was now a military zone, a staging area for IDF operations in the Gaza Strip. The kibbutzim along the border were eerie ghost towns pockmarked by rockets.

Maybe if I stood where my niece and her husband had died and visited the places where Abigail had been kidnapped and her siblings had hidden for fourteen hours, I would discover emotions of anger or sadness or resignation that I hadn't yet let myself feel.

What I was seeking was the opposite of closure: I knew that there would be hard work ahead for me back in the US, where I planned on continuing my work on hostage advocacy. I wanted to speak out against the post–October 7 eruption of anti-Semitism that had pained and deeply unsettled so many American Jews. I had to see the destruction with my own eyes, the places where Hamas terrorists had raped, tortured, killed, and kidnapped innocent civilians, to ensure that reality could never be denied.

When I revisited the time I spent advocating for Abigail and the other hostages, the firmest thing I could grasp was a fifty-one-day haze of constant, numbing anxiety, punctuated with sleepless nights and waking hours where I could barely breathe. Fear, outrage, hopelessness, and anger all blended together, producing spikes of cortisol that at least got me through the most urgent tasks. For those seven weeks, I desperately needed to feel that I was doing everything I possibly could to save Abigail. Now that this first and most vital priority had been accomplished, I needed to cultivate a cooler head and different habits of mind if I wanted to continue to be effective in advocating for the hostages and beleaguered Jewish people over a much longer span of time.

Perhaps my work would have a different tone and urgency once I visited the origin point of our nightmare and saw what Hamas had done to my family's home—a community I felt deeply connected to, and which had once represented the best of what Israel could be. The only way to know what effect this ruined place would have on me was to go and see it.

***

The entrance to Kfar Aza was exactly as I remembered it—the turnoff, the gate, the sign welcoming you to the kibbutz. The tall eucalyptus and palm trees stood there unruffled. The footpaths of the kibbutz were empty, except for the occasional soldier or police officer. I remembered the kibbutz's children playing in a field where Hamas commandos had landed in hang gliders.

The first burned-out house I saw had absorbed a direct RPG strike on October 7, just off the community's main parking lot. Around it was the litter of a disemboweled home: concrete, drywall, pulverized furniture, wads of books and clothing. Across the lot stood a column of IDF soldiers, while Israeli artillery cracked in the distance, louder than any thunder I'd ever heard. A helicopter gunship loitered in the sky high over our heads. Kfar Aza was in a war zone now.

My guides were an IDF public affairs officer and a representative from the Interior Ministry, who advised me to put on a helmet and a heavy vest. We began our tour in the most ruined part of Kfar Aza, the row of bungalow apartments where single young people lived. Black-fringed craters gutted the sidewalks. The structures were in such states of destruction and collapse that the once-solid walls were now char-black windows into ended and interrupted lives.

The attackers left no house unscathed. In the places that still resembled homes, there was overturned furniture, bullet holes, rubble, and the heavy, lingering air of death and destruction.

Real violence is nothing like the well-ordered choreography of a high-budget action film, I realized. Kfar Aza was more like the set of a B movie—the aftermath of a frenzy of violent, hate-fueled chaos, perpetrated by a group of human beings high on bloodlust and the license to murder a community of innocent men, women and children. This was not a movie set, though. It was my family's home, a place I'd been visiting for much of my life, and where some of my best and most sustaining memories had been made.

I had never had the chance to visit Smadar's new house on the kibbutz. This trip would be my first time there. I knew her family lived in a more recently built neighborhood at the edge of town. Now I could see for myself what that meant. They lived at the end of a line of houses angling towards Gaza, right against the perimeter road surrounding the kibbutz's residential area. Terrorists infiltrating from Gaza would have encountered their house before anyone else's. The only thing separating their home from the Gaza border fence, with its inevitably false promise of security, was a quarter mile of fields and a strip of asphalt.

From their front yard you could see the nearby outskirts of Gaza City, now blanketed in a cloud of black smoke. Smadar and Roee could see the homes of their future murderers from their kitchen. Their killers, meanwhile, had rampaged through a village they could see from their own homes.

October 7 had been an intimate event, I realized. It was a close-quarters massacre of neighbor against neighbor. Hamas had exploited the advantage of their closeness to the border communities, using trusted Gazans who worked at the kibbutz as sources of intelligence. They told the attackers about the locations of safe rooms in individual houses, and they even knew which vehicles routinely had keys in them so that they could be used to carry hostages into Gaza City. Hamas had turned the physical proximity of the kibbutzim, and the devotion of many of their residents to strengthening peace and cooperation between the two sides, into some of their deadliest weapons. Many kibbutz members had opened their homes to Gazan workers and had volunteered to bring Gazans who needed medical care to hospitals inside Israel. Their humanitarian instincts had been inverted by their foe into an opportunity for a genocidal rampage.

Every house in the kibbutz had a small wooden sign announcing which family lived there. Abigail's family's sign was still up.

Smadar and Roee had been among the first victims of the attack, but the lawn where Roee had died with Abigail in his arms gave no evidence of an atrocity. The only thing amiss on the façade of the house was the multicolored spray paint on either side of the front door, indicating what various Israeli rescue, bomb-disposal, and cleanup teams had found inside the house. Nearly every house in Kfar Aza had various combinations of this grim graffiti. On the Edans' façade, someone had spray-painted a circle, indicating that a dead body had been found inside.

I walked to the front door, took a breath, and went in.

Time had stopped inside this house at 6:30 a.m. on October 7, 2023. The interior of the house, which bore signs of a chaotic and violent attack, was also full of unfinished actions no one would ever complete. There were dishes in the sink. Little children's shoes were neatly placed near the front door. Toothbrushes and toothpaste were scattered on the bathroom counters. The stillness in the house was an eerie one.

The closet where Michael and Amalia hid in terror for fourteen hours next to their mother's dead body was just beyond the kitchen.

I could see the smoke rising over Gaza, and I could feel the bombs when they struck the ground across the border. Machine guns chattered—every sensory input connected to panic, suffering, and a world gone horribly wrong. The house was only so still because my niece and her family weren't there to fill it with life, and never would be again. I stood in the kitchen alone.

For a moment I felt the weight of everything that had been lost—the absence of lives cut short, the sundering of a place and a family.

I had cried plenty since October 7, but I didn't cry while standing in that house. If I broke down, I wouldn't be able to stand seeing the rest of the kibbutz, and I wouldn't fully remember or process what I'd actually seen. I had to remain stoic, or else it would all be unbearable.

I visited my niece Leron's house and the room where seven people had hidden out from Hamas for twenty-nine hours, including a one-month-old baby. It was dark and cold but uncannily intact in comparison to other houses in their area, most of whose inhabitants had been killed or kidnapped. Standing outside their home, I was overwhelmed to think how close I had been to losing them too.

By the time we got to my sister-in-law Shlomit's house, the abandoned home of someone who had lived in Kfar Aza for nearly six decades, I could barely hear the voices of those accompanying me. After an hour of seeing and feeling the full reality of this tragedy firsthand, it felt like everything around me now was happening at a great distance. The vest weighed heavy on my body, and my heart and soul underneath it felt even heavier. *Where was I? What was I experiencing?* I was comforted by the thought that answers might come later, and that I couldn't possibly get to them if I'd never seen all of this.

Months later, Leron told me a story. She had done a load of laundry on the evening of October 6 of her favorite clothes. The next day, before she could move them into the dryer, the attack had begun. Later, when she returned to the kibbutz, she peered into the machine where the clothing had been left. She didn't imagine they'd be in good shape. But she also didn't expect what she found: a mound of pulverized mush, the rotting and scrambled remnants of a life that didn't exist anymore.

Kfar Aza was the site of some of the worst atrocities human beings can commit against one another. Some of the victims were members of my family. I realized while walking through the burned-out housefronts that it isn't all that helpful to just point out the existence of an evil thing. I had to do something with what I had seen. I had to try to fight this evil, to help limit its power to destroy more lives.

***

But the job that faced me back in America was in some ways harder than it had been before Abigail's release. Most of the youngest hostages, who were the hardest for Hamas to hold and whose kidnappings were the most impossible to digest, had been released during the November ceasefire, which meant that the dynamics of the hostage issue would inevitably shift.

The fate of the hostages always threatened to become less urgent, to fade from general awareness or be overtaken by other wartime issues like the suffering of Gazan civilians, rising anti-Semitism in the United States and around the world, or the looming specter of a full-scale conflict between Israel and Hezbollah in Lebanon. I arrived back in America with a keen sense of how badly we needed to break through the noise and how little time we might actually have left to press our case.

We had a series of important meetings in the days after I got back from Israel. During a busy week back in Washington, the hostage families met with leading senators, CIA Director Bill

Burns, Secretary of State Antony Blinken, and United States president Joe Biden.

Still, not even the United States had the power to fully disentangle the geopolitical nightmare that separated them from their loved ones. On December 12, hostage families met with Tammy Duckworth, Richard Blumenthal, Joni Ernst, Susan Collins, Chris Coons, and others.

I had been in dozens of meetings like these by now. In each new telling of Abigail's story, I spoke as if everyone was hearing it for the first time, and as if I were telling it for the first time. I compartmentalized in order not to grow emotionally numb through the sheer repetition of its horrific details, but I could never treat anything lightly or skip over anything important.

With my own relative released, the story now had a new chapter, one that reminded powerful listeners of what they accomplished before and could accomplish again. I told the senators about getting to hug Abigail, about seeing and embracing this living, breathing proof that it was possible to get the hostages out, if only people like them could exert the right pressure and political will. I wanted to convey a message of hope, and reinforce that another deal that would free the family members of these people who were now part of my extended family was possible.

The next day, our families went to CIA headquarters in Virginia, a place where very few Americans ever get to go. After a few rounds of security checkpoints, with our phones and belongings now secured in lockers, we entered the citadel. We were led down endless stretches of blank walls until we reached a vast and equally featureless conference room where Bill Burns, veteran diplomat and director of the CIA, was waiting for us.

Burns is a soft-spoken power broker, someone who has spent thirty years at the very top of the US foreign policy establishment becoming the intimate of a half-dozen presidents from both parties. He has also been the Biden administration's top negotiator throughout the Hamas hostage crisis. If Biden is the agenda-setter and the embodiment of American conscience and power, and if Jake Sullivan is the strategist tasked with figuring out how to manifest Biden's values and priorities in a complex and often hostile world, Burns is the implementer—the one who sits opposite Qatari, Egyptian, and Israeli counterparts across countless frustrating and repetitive attempts to secure the hostages' freedom. During our meeting, he spoke about the hostage talks with the firsthand knowledge and gravitas of a direct participant. He spoke about his wife and daughters, and about how his own loved ones were a daily reminder of the stakes of bringing the hostages home. Burns told us that his family talked about the hostages at home nearly every day.

The hostage families came with questions that the CIA director wasn't allowed to answer. He couldn't share any of the parties' negotiating redlines. Nor could he give us any real timetable for when talks might succeed, and he couldn't assure us that they would succeed. The US was not directly negotiating with Hamas, and the American assessments of Sinwar—his location, his overall state of mind, his outlook on the war and the hostages—were too sensitive for someone like Burns to share with our group. If some of the hostage families had notions of how they imagined the hostage negotiations should go, Burns politely brought them back to reality. Our meeting became an exercise in expectation management, a preview of the hard months ahead.

After the meeting concluded, I thanked Burns for his work bringing Abigail back to our family—he was one of the people who had negotiated for my great-niece's freedom. For these few private moments, the CIA director's softer, paternal side came out. He expressed his joy in Abigail's release and even told me how personally concerned he was on the first two days of the ceasefire when this beautiful little girl wasn't released from Hamas captivity. America's top intelligence chief is stereotyped as being one of the least sentimental people in government, but Burns is anything but heartless, and the world is much more than a chessboard for him.

***

The American hostage families are a group of intense and outspoken people brought together by different versions of the same unbearable tragedy. We shared the common purpose of trying to save our loved ones from a place of deprivation, pain, torture, abuse, and death. There was no one who wasn't prepared to yell, scream, beg, or strictly discipline themself in order to increase the odds of a miracle.

A bond formed between us out of our pursuit of a shared goal, despite our different backgrounds and emotional makeups and our differing expectations about what could or should happen to our loved ones on any given day. We all knew what the other members of the group were going through. If someone fell apart, there were hands at the ready to pick them up. We became, if not always a unified team working together in harmony, then perhaps something more like a Jewish family—at times fractious, and at other times impossible, but never cold to each other, and always willing to work harder.

Rachel Goldberg-Polin spoke forcefully at the U.N. and the march in Washington for the release of her twenty-three-year-old son Hersh. Single-minded in the pursuit of her son's freedom, accompanied by her steadfast husband Jon, and surrounded by a band of dedicated friends and supporters, she carries herself with a sense of purpose and gravity.

Ruby Chen, whose son Itay disappeared into Gaza on October 7, and whom the Israeli government later determined to have been murdered that day, can be emotional and demanding in meetings, veering off-script—which is sometimes exactly what's needed. He has almost bottomless energy to fight for his son and the other hostages.

Andrea Weinstein, a Connecticut woman whose sister Judih Weinstein was kidnapped, would often read one of Judih's inspired haikus when she got the chance to speak. We later found out Judih and her husband Gadi had been murdered on October 7 while out on an early morning walk, and their bodies were taken to Gaza.

Jonathan Dekel-Chen, a historian of twentieth-century Eastern European Jews at Hebrew University, whose son Sagui, the father of three little girls, was kidnapped, came from nearby Kibbutz Nir Oz and could speak with the sadness and authority of a powerful writer and intellect whose community had experienced some of the day's greatest devastation.

We were a group of American Jews burdened with a tragic and sometimes impossible-seeming mission that we never dreamed of having, pushed to the limits of what the human mind and spirit can reasonably endure.

In the East Wing of the White House, we were all herded into yet another conference room, this one somewhat warmer and less anonymous-seeming than the one at the CIA building in McLean—though notably smaller. The world's most famous mansion is a strangely intimate place.

There was one former hostage among us: Aviva Siegel, a South African–born woman whose husband, the American-born Keith, was still in Hamas captivity. Aviva, also from Kfar Aza, had been released the same day as Abigail and had held my great-niece in her arms as the Red Cross van crept towards Israel. I showed her a picture of Abigail's new family, in which she was smiling alongside her old and new siblings. Aviva had been a nursery school teacher to Leron's twins when they were younger.

We were all chatting when the Secret Service entered. A minute later, the president of the United States walked in.

Biden, who was joined by Secretary of State Antony Blinken, greeted each family individually as he made his way around the room, listening as each one told the story they had come to tell, even if they were ones he clearly already knew. Biden listened as Aviva recalled the hell of being a Hamas hostage. I thanked him for the miracle of Abigail's release and gave him a photograph of Abigail and her family.

After an hour, an aide arrived and told Biden that a group of businessmen and economists were next on his schedule. "Well, they can wait," the president replied, before turning back to us: "You all wanna come with me to the Oval Office?" Biden invited us to walk with him.

I quickly joined the president in the hallway while the other hostage family members were still getting up. I thanked him again and said: "You realize that these people have nobody in Israel like you. There's nobody taking care of them." I wanted

Biden to know that he was, for the time being, the only hope that these people would see their loved ones again.

I could tell that he knew what I was talking about. Israel's leaders often seemed caught between their desire to appease the United States and the political calculations that rule the piranha tank in which Israeli politicians of all parties must swim. Israel's generals were torn between their fear of looking weak in front of their not-so-friendly neighbors and their fear of seeming like monsters in front of their Western counterparts, many of whom had thankfully never had to confront the realities of killing innocent civilians in war and losing hundreds of their best in battle. Behind all of these fears and desires stood the terror state of Iran, which was continuing its rapid pursuit of nuclear weapons, with which it pledged to wipe the Jewish state off the map.

As real as they were, and continue to be, Israel's many problems and challenges could hardly be solved all at once, whether by American diplomacy or through their own military force. Meanwhile, scores of hostages were alive and could still be saved. Biden knew his role was to pressure Hamas and Israel towards the kind of outcome that they'd never agree to on their own. Only he could do that. If he didn't do it, it wouldn't happen. As the famous sign that President Harry S. Truman put on his desk read: "The Buck Stops Here."

Suddenly, the president of the United States was showing us around the world's most famous office. He took photos with us in front of the Resolute Desk. He showed us the side office where he reviews speeches and other important documents. He spoke about the joy of having his late mother onstage with him in Chicago the night he was first elected vice president, fifteen years earlier. Amazingly, he served chocolate chip cookies from the White House kitchen. (I'm a vegan, so I had to decline the offer, but I can tell you they smelled delicious.) There were no aides present, and even Blinken left after a while.

It was vintage Biden, with the warmth of a real, relatable person fused to the heavy responsibilities of leading the most powerful country on Earth. He spent an hour and a half with our families, which is a significant amount of time for any president to spend on anything. He wouldn't have done it if he didn't think it was important.

As a leader and as a human being, Biden believed he needed to see and hear these people who were at the center of the Middle Eastern maelstrom, a crisis that occupied a good part of the attention of the government he led and of his own time. Meanwhile, the hostage families needed to know that he thought about them, cared about them, saw them as real human beings, and was on their side, even though they couldn't always be sure that was true of the Israeli government. It was a powerful and encouraging message.

Still, as we faced the corps of reporters in the post-meeting press conference outside the White House, I was careful not to seem too optimistic, or to let the pomp and ceremony, and the nice treatment, get in the way of why we were all here. We had seen the release of 105 women and children, but there were still over 130 hostages remaining in Gaza.

"I want to remind everyone that these aren't just hostages we were here to talk about," I said. "They're mothers. They're children. They're sons and daughters, husbands and wives and grandparents. They're Americans. They're us."

***

Three days after my meetings with Burns and Biden, I went to Chappaqua, New York, to meet a global figure, who also happens to be a friend and mentor.

Very few people in American public life have been a greater target for a longer period of time than Hillary Clinton. The Republicans put her through a twenty-year gauntlet of investigations and smears. She's had every aspect of her public and personal life scrutinized before the entire planet. Yet I have never seen her bitter, and she is not the kind of person who complains about the past. She was as bright and friendly that afternoon as she was when I'd first met her nearly thirty years earlier, when her astonishing public career was still in front of her.

Hillary Clinton is also a key figure in the history of the modern Middle East, having been first lady during Arafat's rejection of a peace offer at the 2000 Camp David Summit and secretary of state during the Arab Spring and the 2012 Hamas operation. She knows how frustrating the region can be. Yasser Arafat and Yitzhak Rabin were not historical figures for her but people she'd actually known. Having lunch with her, talking about her grandkids and how Abigail and her siblings were doing, helped put my own challenges into much-needed perspective. I gave her a copy of the framed picture of Abigail with her family and thanked her for helping spread awareness of my great-niece's story from the moment we found out she had been taken hostage.

Whenever I talked about the challenges and frustration of the hostage release advocacy, Hillary would remind me that the best response, maybe the only response, is to keep going and to keep doing. It had been over three weeks since the previous hostage deal, with no sign of when the next one would be, or if there would even be one. It was just the message I needed to hear.

***

As December went on, I realized that I didn't feel like being alone on New Year's Eve. What I wanted most was to go back to Israel and to see my family again.

When I arrived in Israel, the new family of eight was making plans to move out of Karen and Dori's house and into something more permanent. Everyone was still struggling, but all they could do was try to move forward and create a routine.

I didn't intend for my second post–October 7 trip to Israel to become an advocacy mission. I'd wanted a break from constant meetings and politics. Somehow, we found each other anyway.

Senators Mark Warner, Kirsten Gillibrand, Lindsey Graham, Mark Kelly, Joni Ernst, Ted Budd, and others were all in the country on congressional delegations. Also at this time, Secretary of State Antony Blinken met with American families in Israel, and even went outside the hotel after our meeting to greet Israeli hostage families.

On top of that, an intriguing opportunity developed through Jay Footlik, the Washington-based lobbyist for the Qatari government. He put me in touch with Eytan Stibbe, a soft-spoken Israeli who made billions through his mostly Africa-focused import-export business and who had traveled to outer space as a tourist. He had his own airplane, which was about to leave for Doha with a number of other Israeli and American hostage family members onboard, including my friends Ruby Chen and Ronen Neutra, as well as a cousin of the kidnapped Bibas family—two little children, one-year-old Kfir Bibas and his brother Ariel, not yet five, were still hostages in Gaza with their parents, Shiri and Yarden.

When a plane travels between Israel and a country that does not have official relations with the Jewish state, it must land in Jordan and refile its flight plans, effectively laundering the aircraft's itinerary. This flight was a very rare exception—we flew all the way to Doha without the required layover. The Qataris wanted to show the utmost respect to the hostage families and did not want the region's political absurdities to get in the way of their humanitarian mission.

We were treated exceptionally well when we got to Qatar's futuristic capital. We were plied with fancy dates and strong, Gulf-style coffee before we even left the airport. At our hotel, Timmy Davis, the US ambassador to Qatar, was there to meet us. Davis is a tough and serious man, an Arabic-speaking Marine corps veteran of operations in Iraq and the Horn of Africa. He has clearly seen and done things most never will, and his experience has made him a careful and highly professional diplomat.

Our next meeting was something of a surprise. We were whisked to a restaurant in the hills above Doha and taken to a private side room, from which we could see the city's science-fiction skyline and the waters of the Gulf shimmering in a gauzy sunset. Our dining companions were members of the senior Qatari hostage negotiation team. It would be hard to imagine the US or Israeli governments sending a large group of very senior diplomats engaged in such sensitive work to a long and informal meeting with hostage activists. The fact that Qatar doesn't even recognize Israel's right to exist made the dinner all the more remarkable.

We sat around a long table filled with Middle Eastern salads—olives, hummus, falafel, cheeses, flatbread of the highest possible quality. This was followed with plates of grilled chicken and lamb. The diplomats wanted us to feel welcome and comfortable as we discussed some inherently painful and frustrating topics. We told our stories, but the negotiators already knew them. One of them had traveled to Israel multiple times and told us about his favorite neighborhoods in Tel Aviv. They told us that the IDF's military campaign made it harder to reach Hamas's Gaza-based leadership, but they did not openly trash the Jewish state or attempt in any way to justify Hamas's actions.

These Qataris were men who were clearly equal to the mind-boggling complexities of their job. They had to keep up relations with Israeli diplomats and intelligence officials that they couldn't publicly talk about—and at the same time they were responsible for keeping a line of communication with Yahya Sinwar, who was hidden away in a tunnel and didn't use a cell phone or computer, but was controlling the entire situation on behalf of Hamas. They had to deal with the Israelis and Americans asking them in private to host the Hamas political leadership, and also with the Israelis and Americans trashing them in public for hosting the Hamas political leadership. These diplomats spoke with remarkable calm about this difficult and sometimes aggravating basket of tasks. I sensed that these were people with admirably small reserves of ego.

The next day we met with Prime Minister Sheikh Mohammed bin Abdulrahman bin Jassim Al Thani, who is also Qatar's minister of foreign affairs. He sat in a throne-like chair in a conference room where the floors were polished to an icy glaze and where servers ensured that we were never out of the strong, traditional coffee that flows freely during meetings in the Gulf. In the presence of this senior royal, one is acutely reminded of the fact that Qatar is a monarchy, and that everyone serves at the pleasure of a single, all-powerful family. I thanked Al Thani for his hard work bringing Abigail home and acknowledged how influential he was in freeing this little child. I was astonished when I looked up and saw that he was crying.

There is much legitimate criticism to be made of Qatar, which has gotten itself in trouble by trying to play every side of every Middle Eastern conflict. Yet the ability to host both the Hamas high command and the US Sixth Fleet reflects considerable political sophistication, if also moral incoherence.

Qatar is not an open or democratic place. But as we were ushered around Doha, I saw a city that looked as if each of the world's greatest and most imaginative architects had been given a free hand to design the skyscraper of their choice. I saw one of the world's great Islamic art museums, housed in an I.M. Pei–designed artificial island in Doha's bay. The Qatari capital had a glittering new metro system and airport. It had just hosted the World Cup. It had everything a cutting-edge major city should have.

A few months later, I would be invited to attend a global security conference in Doha with Yael Alexander, the mother of twenty-year-old American hostage Edan Alexander, a young man who grew up in New Jersey and was abducted from a base along the Gaza border. During the conference, I spoke onstage with Roger Carstens about the role our American hostage families played in the framework of US hostage affairs. It was a unique opportunity to tell Abigail's story and that of all the hostages, in front of an audience who depended on Al Jazeera for their news.

In the face of all this growth and wealth, it was hard not to imagine an alternate reality in which the Palestinians of Gaza had given themselves the opportunity to use the many billions of dollars poured into their coffers over many decades by Western governments, Arab countries, and U.N. agencies to build modern skyscrapers instead of an underground city of tunnels. The Gaza Strip has objectively nicer beaches than Doha. It is more centrally located, filling the coastline that connects Egypt, the Arab world's most populous country, to Israel, the most open society in the Middle East.

It's hard not to think about what the Gazans could have if they one day fought for a different future, one in which their home isn't a giant terror fortress, and where they aren't pawns of a psychopath hiding 250 feet below the earth—someone who uses every available mosque, hospital, and school to pervert the minds of children and adults alike into hating their neighbors, and who then trains them to murder without conscience, in God's name. A better reality is possible—which makes the current one such a tragic waste.

7

I was awestruck at what Capitol Hill is like the night of the State of the Union. The US federal government, one of the most powerful and confounding entities in the history of the world, is suddenly compressed into the intimate confines of the House chamber.

Each family member of an American hostage was invited by a specific member of Congress. I was the guest of Congresswoman Haley Stevens, an energetic leader from Michigan who also serves on the bipartisan Congressional Task Force on American Hostages. The family members in attendance all wore yellow scarves, to bring attention to our plight.

In the Visitors' Gallery, we could see the entire senior leadership of the United States government. Supreme Court justices, cabinet secretaries, agency chiefs, and congressional power brokers gathered below us and then rose as the president, vice president, and speaker of the House took their places at the rostrum.

The president stood up and began his biggest address of the year. The contrast between the relatively small space and the outsized importance of the event made it seem like the president was speaking to everyone individually. There were only two instances throughout the hour-long speech where the entire Republican side of the room joined their Democratic colleagues in a unanimous, bipartisan standing ovation. The first time was to commemorate the memory of John Lewis, the icon of the civil rights movement who served in Congress for thirty-two years before his death in 2020. The second time was to support the freedom of the hostages held by Hamas.

The sparse amount of shared applause was sad evidence of American polarization, but it also reflected the hostage families' larger strategy of bipartisanship. At a time when Democrats and Republicans often view each other as threats to the entire country—as enemies, almost—we had maintained a bipartisan consensus around the need for a hostage deal. The hostage families had kept the issue as something that transcended politics, and we'd done this because we hadn't become partisans ourselves.

I ran into Secretary of State Antony Blinken in a corridor after the speech. "Thank you for what you're doing and for your leadership. It's really important," America's top diplomat told me. "There's no rest until we get them out," I told him.

The evening at the Capitol reminded me that a hostage deal wasn't some outlandish or extreme prospect, even after all these months of stasis, and even though we had not seen any movement on a deal since the temporary ceasefire that brought Abigail back to our family had broken down at the beginning of December. We kept returning to D.C. to meet with the congressional leaders and the White House teams, in hopes that our pressure and our presence would save the lives of our loved ones, who had been held in captivity by Hamas for four and a half months at this point.

Over the course of January and February, we learned that the US had hammered out a basic framework for a deal, one that the parties had accepted in various unofficial forms. Israel would dial down its military campaign in three phases, during which different categories of hostages would be released: the remaining children first, followed by the elderly, young women and female soldiers, followed by other men and active-duty soldiers, followed by dead bodies, which would be released in the final phase. Israel and Hamas had to determine a hostage-to-prisoner release ratio, and the Israelis still had to agree on which aspects of the war they were willing to suspend, or end altogether, at each given phase of the agreement.

Hamas was demanding that Israel withdraw its military, agree to a permanent ceasefire, and allow for the multibillion-dollar reconstruction of the Strip, conditions that Israeli leaders viewed as a demand for surrender. Israel wanted to be able to keep some of its troops in Gaza and wanted Hamas to agree to relinquish power over the Strip. There were signs of flexibility in Hamas's position. At one point, there was hope that female active duty IDF soldiers taken captive would be grouped with young female civilians. We knew women were raped and abused in captivity from other hostages who had returned in the first release at the end of November. It is unclear if Hamas ever accepted this part—and if they did, it wasn't enough to bring a deal to life—but in the context of a hostage negotiation, it can be a source of hope when a compromise isn't shot down entirely.

A hostage deal could have been greatly helped along if the International Committee of the Red Cross had made any effort whatsoever to access the hostages, to determine which of the Hamas captives were even still alive, and perhaps to administer basic medical help and medication—lists of which were provided to the ICRC by desperate family members. In a late November meeting with ICRC officials in Washington, not long after Abigail was freed, American hostage family members, including myself, were told that making such basic demands of Hamas would only antagonize the Gaza Strip's jihadist authorities. I remarked that the Red Cross needed to be more than a dysfunctional Uber service out of Gaza for hostages. I then reminded the officials that ICRC staff were the first people to see the hostages, many of them little children, upon their release, and could see for themselves how emaciated, pale, and generally mistreated they were.

The ICRC's refusal to do its job, and its dehumanizing failure to even try to advocate that these hostages be treated like prisoners of war, let alone as the innocent civilians most of them were, greatly bolstered Hamas's bargaining position. They were careful not to reveal which of the hostages were alive—Americans and Israelis could never be totally sure they weren't negotiating over dead bodies. In one back-and-forth, Hamas changed the wording of the agreement to allow itself to choose whether to release living hostages or corpses. The ICRC failed to uphold its mandate and enabled Hamas's psychological warfare. When the group released a video of Hersh Goldberg-Polin, who had lost his left arm in a grenade attack on October 7, it was his parents' first proof of their son's life since his kidnapping.

Thankfully, Abigail was no longer a hostage. She was now safe. I continued in my role as an advocate but dialed down my activities as a spokesperson in the press. The media wanted stories of raw suffering that I could no longer provide.

Viewers were understandably interested in Abigail's experiences in captivity and her new life after her ordeal in Gaza. What had she eaten? Had she been abused? Where was she living? What did she say about her fifty-one days in captivity? I wanted to protect my Israeli family's privacy during a sensitive moment and keep Abigail safe from the intrusive glare of the media.

But the Israeli-American hostage families continued to make a powerful moral and strategic case that the US government needed to do all it could to free our loved ones. We had to keep the pressure up for a hostage agreement, but we had to do it without politicizing the situation. We had to keep a united public front for the eight Americans and the other hostages still captive in Gaza.

Predictably, differences of opinion between the hostage families would surface whenever some new figure tried to come onboard to help. Mickey Bergman represented an especially thorny case. Bergman was the Israeli-born, Virginia-based top operative for the late governor and U.N. Ambassador Bill Richardson, who made hostage affairs his signature issue after he left government in the 2000s. Bergman and Richardson had a record of success and controversy together—some of their more notable cases included helping to free two American journalists from North Korean captivity a decade ago and the deal to free basketball star Brittney Griner from Putin's Russia. At the same time, they had attracted criticism for negotiating with rogue regimes and terror groups outside of official channels. Both men were viewed as being close to the Qatari government's project of becoming the world's one-stop shop for hostage negotiation. Bergman carried on Richardson's legendary and creative hostage work after his death in September of 2023.

As a private-sector nonprofit officer in contact with top officials in multiple governments, the nature of Bergman's role—along with any real sense of which figures in which governments stand behind him—can be difficult even for insiders to figure out. Personally, I found Bergman to be a very useful resource, an experienced mind that I could bounce ideas off of—someone who is unusually willing to share his unvarnished opinion of where things really stand, and who was always available to help. I also learned that, beyond his gruff exterior, he is a kind and deeply thoughtful person. He provided valuable reality checks in the midst of much confusion.

His advice, however, sometimes clashed with that of SKDK, the Washington-based PR firm, and this could be a source of tension. The important thing was not to allow our differences to blow up into public disagreement, even when private disagreements were inevitable and sometimes even productive.

I could see nerves beginning to fray during a late January meeting in Washington with Jake Sullivan and his top Middle East deputy, the veteran diplomat Brett McGurk. One father of a hostage began to criticize the Biden administration in unusually sharp terms—why weren't our children free yet? What are you all even doing in these endless meetings in Qatar, Paris, and Cairo? And where are the sanctions on Qatar? Why doesn't Qatar kick Hamas out of their capital, Doha? Sullivan explained, with the utmost politeness, that there were things the US government was doing that no one could talk about and that no one, including the family members present, would ever learn about. Even in the hardest moments, Sullivan and McGurk's candor, and their refusal to sugarcoat anything, was appreciated by the hostage families.

At every meeting, he gave each hostage family member a chance to speak, including people he suspected might be critical of him. Jake listened intently, took our ideas seriously, and made sure the mutual respect between the families and American officials never flagged. He didn't shy away from telling us that the core dynamic of the talks remained stubbornly in place, and that a deal, any deal, depended largely on the political will of two people.

After an intense hour, I stepped into my unofficial position as closer. I summed up the conversation we'd just had with Sullivan and McGurk and asked what role we could play in the coming days and weeks to support their efforts; I wanted to make sure that the meeting would end on a proactive and hopeful note. Yet at times like those, I would also despairingly wonder, as I did every morning when I woke up and every night before I fell asleep, whether any of what we did truly mattered.

Perhaps that explains why some of the hostage families were disappointed with the State of the Union address. Biden did not mention any hostage families by name, which I do not believe was intended as any kind of a slight. But the families were and are in a daily state of torment. Any perceived accompanying loss of perspective was a reflection of how heartbreaking and impossible their situations are. They wanted the president to say and do more. But he isn't the president of Israel or of Gaza. He is the president of the United States. His time and attention are limited, even if he was doing everything in his power to make a hostage deal happen.

The families were doing everything they could too. One question haunted them each and every day: *What if it isn't enough?*

***

Some people believe in authorities that are even higher than American presidents, and while I have never been an especially observant Jew, I have always had a sense that appealing to God for help is never a bad idea.

A week after the State of the Union address, I joined Yael and Adi Alexander, as well as Ronen and Orna Neutra, on a trip to the Montefiore Cemetery in eastern Queens to pray for their two boys who had been hostages in Gaza at this point for nearly six months. The cemetery is home to the grave of Menachem Mendel Schneerson, the last Lubavitcher Rebbe and the guiding light of the Chabad Hasidic movement.

Visitors to the Rebbe's resting place are supposed to write their deepest earthly and spiritual wishes on a piece of paper, which they then tear up and cast into the rectangular trench containing his tombstone and burial site. There are always mountains of torn paper heaped atop the grave. Nearby, hundreds of memorial candles melt into one another at every hour of the day. There was nothing about the holy site that felt superstitious, pointless, or excessively pious to me at this time in my life. Throughout this ordeal, I've realized that prayers are a means of cultivating good thoughts and positive energy. The grave was filled with people, some of whom recognized us as hostage families and told us they had been praying for us since October 7. This meant so much to us.

Around this same time, I spoke to college-age women leaders from the right-wing group Concerned Women for America, led by Penny Nance. Most of the activists were Evangelical Christians, like Penny. Each and every one of these bright, young women had led a vigil for the hostages on their campus or had organized to help Jewish students in the wake of October 7. We did not share a religious tradition, and in truth we agreed on very little. But I was greatly moved when they prayed for me, for Abigail, for all the hostages, and for the Jewish people. As I had told the *Christian Post* after Abigail was released, what kept us going was "the incredible outpouring of love and support and prayer from people all over the world, different religions, different races, that have reached out to us and different parts of our family, just to say, 'We're here for you, we're praying for Abigail, we're praying for all of the hostages.'"

At the Rebbe's grave, I thought back to that first Shabbat after October 7, when I'd heard Senator Cory Booker speak at a synagogue in suburban New Jersey. I had just learned that Abigail was likely alive in Hamas captivity, and I was in a state of deep shock. Something incomprehensibly horrible had happened. Smadar was dead along with 1,200 other Israelis, including 40 Americans, and her three-year-old girl was a hostage along with 246 other innocent people. Cory's message, citing the opening lines of the Torah—the "let there be light" that would be read in synagogues around the world that weekend—was that even the deepest evil needed to be a spark for action and eventual optimism.

He was right of course. But at the time I kept thinking: *If there is a God, I am so mad at this being.*

I have a different attitude now. My anger-fueled skepticism in the wake of October 7—how could such a cruel God be worthy of anyone's admiration?—had morphed into a sense that we can use all the help we can get. Even an inchoate sense of a higher power can make us better able to propel ourselves forward against the darkness of an oftentimes cruel and unjust reality.

I also learned that lack of control isn't the same thing as paralysis. I could try to help where I could, repair what could be fixed, and at least keep fighting for something better. And I learned that in my quest I could turn for help to people both expected—like Cory—and surprising, like Penny and others.

***

There was so much work to be done to get the hostages home to their families. There was so much to be done for Abigail too. My Israeli family and I would make sure Hamas hadn't destroyed her life and create the opportunity for all those prayers for her, from all over the world, to be answered.

Once Leron, Zoli, and their new family of eight had established some kind of sustainable routine, it was time to start giving all of them a fresh supply of happy memories and fun experiences. Moving, starting anew, and taking care of the family was a twenty-four-seven job for Leron and Zoli. Getting the children into schools, coordinating government benefits, finding counselors and therapists for everyone, and moving into a permanent new house was hard, draining work.

Zoli now drove all six kids to their various schools every morning. In the late afternoon, when all the kids returned from school and playdates, Zoli and Leron were a tag team, with crucial help from grandmother Shlomit. Zoli ran the kitchen as he had during his many years as a chef and restaurant owner. Leron kept everyone on schedule, doing mountains of laundry, vacuuming, and bathing little ones. Shlomit was an all-around source of love and support. I was in awe of their incredible fortitude, and I was sure that healing was progressing, even with so much tragedy and loss.

In March, I visited them in their new home. I would sit with Leron during the mid-afternoon gap of quiet, when no one else was home. We talked about the kids and how they were holding up, and we often reminisced about her sister and best friend Smadar. Then the kids would get home: Michael, who is more reserved than the rest of them, always gave a warm hug; twelve-year-old Zohar gave the strongest hug. Abigail never missed a chance to crawl on Leron's and Zoli's laps. When they were busy, she would jump in my arms or hold my hand and shout, "Leez, come and play with me!"

I marveled as I watched her making funny expressions during pictures, sticking out her tongue and wrinkling her nose. We'd have to bribe her to give a normal smile in family photos (and she knows how to extract as high a price as possible). She takes and sends selfies, tells people the difference between Coke Zero and other kinds of Coke, and has everyone's phone passwords memorized.

I didn't bring up Smadar with Abigail, although I knew she sometimes talked about her with Leron and Zoli, usually at night as she was being tucked in for bed. On this trip, Abigail boasted to me that her mother could speak Arabic and English, in addition to Hebrew. Abigail then showed me how she could count to ten in all three of Israel's official languages.

In early April, the whole family flew out to visit and stay with me in Los Angeles, the first time they had ever traveled together outside of Israel. After months of terror and uncertainty, this was a special opportunity for this unexpected now-nuclear family to build beautiful and sustaining memories together. A short documentary about them had recently appeared on Uvda, Israel's version of *60 Minutes*. Some on their flight out of Tel Aviv recognized this little girl and her family, and a few tweeted in excitement about being on the same plane with them—people who now represented not just terror but also glimmers of hope.

Getting to know Abigail as a person rather than as an abstraction or the face of an impossible human catastrophe was a profound joy. She has a magnetic personality—she's the kind of little kid people like being around, even without them knowing what she's been through. She's a generous hugger and huge cuddler, and it's sometimes impossible to get her to stop dancing and jumping.

She had fun splashing in the freezing water of Malibu beach and running around Legoland with her five siblings. She biked and swam and got her first real mani-pedi. I learned that she has a massive sweet tooth and loves fruit. She is always up for French fries. Her favorite Israeli staple is chicken schnitzel. She loves strawberry ice cream. I had the privilege of giving Abigail her first churro, which she also loved.

While usually in her own world of being a child, she's also really smart—sharp and subtle the way Smadar was at her age.

She's so smart that I sometimes worry she understands too much about what has happened to her.

In the middle of the family's visit to Los Angeles, I flew to D.C. for meetings. That week, the American hostage families were invited to meet with Vice President Kamala Harris. The vice president greeted each family member personally and warmly as she made her way around the room. Then she took her seat at the head of the table. She listened intently to each member share their thoughts and promised to keep working with the president to bring our loved ones home, as well as to find resolutions to the fighting in Gaza. Dean Lieberman and Rebecca Lissner, the vice president's deputy national security advisors, and Erin Wilson, the vice president's deputy chief of staff, who had met with us in November, were also there with Phil Gordon, Lorraine Voles, and Brett McGurk. After the meeting, the vice president and her team spent time speaking individually with all of our families before departing.

Right after the meeting, I was back on the plane to Los Angeles. My daughters and I joined the family for a trip to the greatest monument of childhood, Disneyland, a much-loved staple of my own childhood. Abigail met Daisy and Donald Duck and rode on the flying Dumbos. She loved the "Cars" ride so much that we went on it twice in a row, jetting through a dreamlike mockup of the Arizona desert in a fake convertible. On the Pirates of the Caribbean ride, I was reminded that Abigail is still sensitive to stimuli that might remind her of Gaza. I could feel how scared the cannon blasts and the darkness made her and was angry at myself for not thinking of her likely reactions ahead of time. I was touched when I saw twelve-year-old Inbar grasp her hand and gently explain that it wasn't real.

Her favorite ride of the day was It's a Small World. Abigail got up and danced, right there in our slow-moving boat, and her eyes expanded into spheres of wonder as she gazed upon the little continents of singing and swaying children, arrayed in a 1950s ideal of what their homelands and national dress were supposed to look like.

Maybe, I thought, one day she'd get to see many of the real-life versions of the places depicted in the ride. Maybe the peoples of the world might all get along with each other and help make the world better, together. That wasn't what we were living through now.

The trauma of the past few months will always be there, I realized, but it hadn't canceled out the prospect of a happy future. Abigail had been through something unimaginable, and she couldn't avoid its consequences over the course of her life. But thankfully, now Abigail had her whole life ahead of her. Whatever lay ahead, for that one day she was like any other kid, awestruck at the Sleeping Beauty Castle and the magical Main Street parade, even if she'd been places and seen things that no other kid at Disneyland had.

The family's next stop was New York. It was the week of Passover, when Jews celebrate our emancipation from slavery in Egypt. We weren't really in the mood for the holiday. Leron missed her sister and was nostalgic for Passover in Kfar Aza. We decided to have a simple family dinner. The one tradition we did follow was to search for the afikomen, the piece of unleavened bread whose discovery is supposed to symbolize the Jews' final redemption and every child's favorite part of the Passover Seder.

The kids enjoyed taking rowboats on the lake in Central Park and crossing the harbor on the Staten Island Ferry. Leron and the kids loved shopping for new clothes, and Michael was thrilled to go to Dunkin' Donuts, a place his father had told him about. Taking the New York subway was a ride on par with the ones at Disneyland—for the kids, at least. The days were full, and they flew by as I rediscovered the city through their young eyes.

Midway through the New York leg of their trip, we were all supposed to meet Hillary Clinton at her office at Columbia University. I was looking forward to taking the family to the landmark Ivy League campus. But in the latest expression of hate set off by the violence of October 7, the campus had been shut down. Butler Library's front lawn now hosted an encampment of anti-Israel protesters, whose residents called for a ceasefire on the one hand, while voicing support for continuing violence against Israelis and discrimination against Jewish students. This encampment included both students and members of radical groups—part of a series of global protests in support of a Hamas victory. All around the world, thousands of people chanted "from the river to the sea," wearing keffiyehs, the green headband of Hamas, even brandishing the flag of Iranian-sponsored Hezbollah.

Where I live, these protests had tried to shut down everything from airports and train stations to the Rockefeller Center Christmas Tree lighting ceremony to a children's cancer hospital—as well as college campuses throughout New York. Our meeting with Clinton was first delayed, then finally relocated to another one of the former secretary of state's offices in midtown.

Huma Abedin, Clinton's longtime aide, met us on the ground floor. Upon seeing Abigail, a look of awe and surprise spread across the face of this senior diplomat. (Abedin asked the kids if they knew who Hillary Clinton was. One of the twins said, "President Clinton's wife." Huma and I laughed. "Wrong answer," I said.)

Leron especially looked forward to thanking Hillary for calling her mother, Shlomit, on the day Smadar was buried. Hillary spoke with the kids, asking them about their time in New York.

The former secretary of state had been by our family's side since October 7. In a way, she had been in our family's life for decades—since the time I first heard my own father mention her husband's name as an up-and-coming voice in American politics. To be able to celebrate Abigail's freedom with Hillary, whose advice and encouragement had been so invaluable, was a moment I'll never forget.

***

"Thank God she is home," President Biden said in a press conference the day that Abigail was released. "I just can't imagine the joy."

The president's team had made it known to me that Biden wanted to meet with the family when they came to the States.

I rented a Sprinter van for the day of April 24. The whole family, along with my daughter Noa, woke up before dawn for the four-hour drive down I-95. Eleven tired and excited travelers piled into the van. A traffic jam we hit just before arriving in D.C. threatened to make us late, but we used it as a chance to change into our White House clothes in the car and brush (and, in some cases, braid) our hair.

We felt welcomed at the world's most famous and powerful house before we even set foot in the place: after an inspection, White House security let the van drive through the gates and all the way up to the front door—unusual for any visitor arriving in a private vehicle. Then again, I thought for the umpteenth time since the end of November, a four-year-old survivor of a terrorist hostage ordeal is pretty unusual too.

We went on a tour with the White House guide. I carried Abigail through the historic guest rooms and the presidential movie theater. The adults and the older children understood that they were at the epicenter of earthly power, but my great-niece was tired from the trip and kept falling asleep in my arms. I discreetly asked an aide named Evy if she could get something sugary, and she returned in minutes with a supply. After a handful of M&Ms and some cookies, Abigail and the whole family got a strong second wind just in time for our next stop: the Oval Office.

President Biden waited for us alone.

What Biden wanted from his meeting with Abigail and our family was not just a photo opportunity. It was an unmediated experience with people he'd helped, a living reminder of the powers and responsibilities of his office. I wondered if, after months of war in the Middle East and a bruising election season ahead—one in which he would eventually drop his reelection bid—Biden needed to be re-nourished in his work, which can be so thankless and difficult.

The president hugged all six of the children, and they all gave him pictures they'd drawn to thank him. Abigail's was a bubble-shaped, stick-figure portrait of the president getting ready to dig into an ice cream cone. As a four-year-old she did not think of him as "the president," but she knew the name of the grandfatherly man she was meeting: "Joe! Joe!" she yelled out. Biden turned to her, and she gave him a playful pat on the head.

Biden then told the kids about his own story of loss. The president recalled the great trauma of his life, the 1972 car accident in which his wife and daughter were killed. "I know what it's like to have dark days," the president said.

He took us into his smaller private office where he sits alone and writes speeches. He showed us the wall his desk faces, which is full of pictures that other children had drawn and sent to him. He asked the kids if he could put their art on the wall, and all six of them nodded in proud agreement.

Then Biden started telling the children another, happier story. "There was a famous president named John F. Kennedy," he said to the children, "and he had kids who were your age." The six young visitors then took turns reenacting the October 1963 photo of John F. Kennedy Jr. crawling out from under the Resolute Desk and peeking out of a small hatch beneath his hard-at-work father. The image is an icon of the simplicity and innocence of children crossing paths with the grandiosity of American power. A sadder parallel occurred to me, though: Michael, Amalia, and Abigail's father had been murdered, just like JFK Jr.'s would be only a month after that photo was taken.

The meeting then turned into a reunion of the officials who had helped Abigail get out of Gaza and who had been instrumental in saving her life. Jake Sullivan and Brett McGurk arrived, along with David Cotter, the NSC's director for hostage and detainee affairs. "These people helped bring you back from Gaza," I told Abigail. She smiled and gave them a line of leaping high-fives.

Sullivan, not known for showing a ton of emotion, cracked the biggest smile I'd ever seen on him. I remembered the first time we met in November, when I had shared Abigail's story with him, and he had cried. He felt the pain of this tragedy as a human, not just a man with a powerful title and job.

McGurk has spent much of his career working on intractable Middle Eastern conflicts and had invested countless hours in the deal that freed Abigail and scores of other hostages. Cotter had been the intermediary with Jake and Brett, and he was another official who had made himself available twenty-four-seven for me and all the other American hostage families. I could tell that this meeting gave all three of these men a sense of accomplishment and contentment that could otherwise be elusive in their often-thankless line of work.

When the photographer was ready to take a picture of the president and the kids, I placed Abigail on the Resolute Desk, before having immediate second thoughts: I asked the president if this was somehow a violation of presidential protocol.

He smiled, stood proudly, and put his arm around this little child he saved from the grasp of Hamas terrorists, who was now nearly at eye level with him. The two posed for a picture, both of them beaming.

Abigail had been a hostage for fifty-one days, a child whom terrorists had crammed into a succession of dark rooms in Gaza after murdering her parents. Now she was in a bright and hopeful place, the president's office, perched on the desk where the world's great decisions were made.

Next the president invited the children to go outside to the White House swing set, which he had installed for his own grandchildren. The kids ran as if they had arrived at a friend's house for a playdate.

Noa and I hung back in the Oval Office with Biden. He looked at us and spoke as if he were not the president but just a man who had learned something about life and wanted to share it with us. He talked about suddenly being left alone with two little boys, both seriously injured from the car accident. His sister and family showed up and never left him alone, not in their darkest days, not even now, when he was president of the United States. He told us that even when it wasn't obvious, our togetherness made all the difference in moving forward. He added: "There will be a time when their memories of their parents will make them smile, and not just cry." We all hugged him. Then he said, "Let's go outside and join the others."

When we exited, the sight we saw made me catch my breath: Abigail was on the White House swings, laughing. She had enlisted Brett McGurk to push her, yelling, "Higher."

President Biden went over to Leron and Zoli and spoke to them for a short while alone. I knew this was a moment where he was just with them and for them—two survivors who were picking up the pieces from this horrific time.

Biden was eventually summoned to a meeting. He offered me some parting words. He was speaking with an authenticity that most Americans no longer expect from our leaders, American politics having become a cynical charade as far as much of the country is concerned. "We have to get the rest of the hostages back," Biden told me before taking his leave. "That is my commitment."

That sense of dedication was something we felt from the entire staff. When we returned, I received a note from the staffer who had coordinated our visit. He shared how meaningful our visit had been for them and how important it was to make sure that Abigail, Michael, Amalia, Leron, and the entire family were able to enjoy ourselves and create a few lasting memories.

***

On May 31, President Biden made a press announcement about a three-stage deal to release the hostages, stop the fighting, surge aid to the Palestinians, and begin to implement the "Day After" plan for Gaza. He framed this as a deal that Netanyahu had recently agreed to in principle, insinuating that the pressure was now on Hamas to accept it. They had agreed to the principles of this deal months before.

Biden was familiar with the dance of both sides: When one side was agreeing, the other side would find problems or ask for new things they wanted. Hamas and Israel could debate the exact IDF withdrawal lines and the precise timetable for hostage releases forever if they weren't pressured into making a real, if mutually risky, decision. An agreement could be days away, or it might never happen at all.

By the time summer rolled around, rumors were swirling that a hostage deal had never been closer. In the latest of their now-regular meetings with American hostage families, Sullivan and McGurk were a bit more optimistic than I'd seen them in months. We knew that both Israel and Hamas had accepted an American framework for a hostage deal, which the U.N. Security Council, the G7, and most major world leaders had also endorsed.

It was in this context that I and the other American hostage families finally met—for the first time since October 7—one of the other major world leaders in whose hands the fate of the remaining hostages lay: Benjamin Netanyahu.

8

The prime minister was in Washington to address a joint session of Congress. I got in touch with Gefen Ahituv, the assistant to Israeli ambassador to the US Michael Herzog, about arranging for the American hostage family members to meet with Netanyahu when he arrived in D.C. a couple of nights before his speech.

American hostage families had never met with Netanyahu as a group. Many of the families were frustrated with him. It had been nearly three hundred days since their loved ones were kidnapped. Some felt he resented our work and believed that our communications with the American government—and the pressure from the American government that we were exacting on the negotiations—complicated his job, distracting attention from the effort to beat back Hamas. A palpable tension had built up between our group and Netanyahu's team, with some American hostage family members debating whether to even attend a meeting with him without American leaders to bear witness to the conversation.

Despite all of this, along with other American hostage families, I kept pushing—calling and writing staff in bipartisan congressional offices to try and arrange this meeting and checking in every couple of days about progress. I worked with Gefen and her colleagues at the embassy. The American families made public statements in the press—but for weeks there was still no response from the prime minister's office.

About a week before Netanyahu's arrival, we learned that President Biden had heard of our efforts, and that his own team started pushing for a meeting at the White House—with *both* him and Netanyahu.

Eventually, Netanyahu's team agreed to a meeting with American hostage families—but without congressional leaders, and with other Israeli hostage families, which felt chaotic and less beneficial. Nevertheless, we decided to take what we could get.

The meeting took place at the legendary Watergate Hotel, which was heavily surrounded by barricades and well-armed police. It was a forbidding environment, and not only for us. Around this time, videos were posted of anti-Israel activists releasing hundreds of mealworms, maggots, and crickets in the hotel—a disgusting "welcome" for the leader of a country under siege since the worst terrorist attack in its history.

Inside, things in our meeting got off on the wrong foot almost immediately. I had been promised that the discussion would be held in English; when I arrived, I was told that this had never been agreed to. I said I didn't want my picture taken there; a close-up of me shaking the prime minister's hand went up on the Israeli news website Ynet almost immediately. We had wanted the meetings just to be with the American hostage families; Netanyahu brought along Israeli hostage families—

including twenty-six-year-old Noa Argamani, who had been kidnapped from the Nova music festival and was one of four hostages rescued in a daring operation in early June.

After greeting all the guests around the table with his wife, Sara, Bibi began by telling the families that he was committed to getting their loved ones home. He said he was doing all he could to get them back and that he would continue to do all he could. Then the families were invited to speak. One religious woman, whose son was being held in Gaza, said that Netanyahu should not be pressured to take a bad deal. One of the American hostage family members talked about the fact that a recent poll said a majority of Israelis prioritized a hostage deal over finishing the war. The room was relatively quiet but the speakers' voices were intense and passionate.

After hearing from many of the hostage families, Gal Hirsch, Netanyahu's hostage envoy, introduced me as Abigail's aunt and invited me to speak, something I hadn't planned on doing. I believe I was the only person in the room who did not have an Israeli passport; plus, my own loved one had already been released. Still, I felt an obligation. My position as a US citizen—and a US citizen only—meant that I was freer than others to speak my mind, to say what others might feel too constrained to say.

I began by welcoming the prime minister and his wife to my country. I told him that both Republicans and Democrats agreed that the hostages must be released—one of the few areas of bipartisan agreement in a polarized time, with a big election nearing.

"I was raised to love Israel," I said. I told him I had lived there and worked there, that I had always believed in the country, and I still believed in it. Then I made my pitch.

"This is a time for brave and bold leadership," I said, and everyone knew what I was referring to. The day before, Joe Biden had announced he would drop out of the presidential race, choosing the national interest over his own personal ambition. "Put your country first," I told Netanyahu. "Israel needs a deal. Israel needs to bring home these hostages. You are the only one who can make this decision, and it is time for you to make it."

Netanyahu had obviously heard this line of argument before, from people who were of much greater political interest to him than I could ever be. Israel was facing an existential danger, he replied. He hinted that taking the wrong hostage deal would be a repeat of the pre–October 7 mentality, in which Israel had been overconfident about its security. The effect of him saying this to a room full of October 7 victims, whose loved ones like my family were murdered and taken hostage, was not positive.

He then said to the suffering families that while they may each have one person they want to save, he has ten million citizens to protect—a statement that, however true, landed like lead. The sensitivity and empathy that we had come to expect from global leaders was absent.

He then launched into a twenty-minute lecture about Hamas, Iran, the implacable position that Israel found itself in, and so on. And with that, the conversation came to an end. "We are closer to a deal than we ever have been," he said, but gave no further details.

After the meeting, I noted to Gal Hirsch that the people in that room had spent nine months working and advocating as Americans to create relationships and establish open communications with government officials including the vice president and the president of the United States. I told him I suspected the content of Netanyahu's remarks would not land well on the ears of these American hostage families. "They are all Israelis," he said, dismissively.

It felt like a competition, when we all should have been on the same side.

***

The next day, while Bibi and his team traversed Capitol Hill, American hostage families did the same.

We held a briefing with New Jersey representative Josh Gottheimer and Illinois representative Brad Schneider, congressional leaders and extraordinary advocates for the hostages. We had a private meeting with House Minority Leader Hakeem Jeffries and his executive director Gideon Bragin; we knew they were seeing Netanyahu later that day, and we urged them to push for a deal in that meeting.

Elisa Catalano Ewers, a friend and senior professional staff member for the Senate Foreign Relations Committee who had arranged the first meeting with the committee back in November, put together a working reception with bipartisan senators and the hostage families. Again, this was useful: many of the leaders in attendance—Senators Cardin, Duckworth, Schumer, Graham, Rosen, Collins, and Ernst—would later be meeting with the prime minister and his team. We also did a round table with the House Foreign Affairs Committee led by Republican Chairman McCaul and Ranking Member Meeks, whose bipartisan committee we had met with at the end of last November.

One of the true achievements of our advocacy for nine months was that we had managed to keep our work bipartisan.

The week before I had traveled to Milwaukee with Orna and Ronen Neutra to attend the Republican National Convention. In the weeks leading up to it, I had asked Penny Nance if I could talk about the hostages at her pink Concerned Women for America bus parked outside the Fiserv Forum. She loved the idea, and I invited the Neutras to join. Then I asked about something else: whether she thought the Neutras could speak at the convention.

To my utter astonishment, Penny made it happen. On Wednesday night, in front of the seventeen thousand people inside the arena and many millions more watching on television, the Neutras spoke to a warm and supportive audience chanting, "Bring Them Home," and waving posters with that saying throughout the crowd. Their message was simple: Eight of the hostages still in Gaza for over 284 days were Americans—and one of them was their son. We all had to do everything to free them.

If you had told me, at any point in my adult life before October 7, 2023, that I would attend the Republican National Convention—let alone that it would bring me to grateful tears—I would have told you that you were nuts. But I've learned since October 7 that although evil can manifest in ways you never expected, so can good people—whatever their politics.

This was the driving impulse behind the advocacy work we did in Washington. To Netanyahu and his team, we may have been just "Israelis," but we knew we were Americans, beating the paths of our own capitol, putting ourselves in rooms we had never imagined, creating relationships we never thought possible—all in a fight for the lives of our loved ones.

***

The following morning, before Netanyahu's address to Congress, a van picked us up from the hotel and drove us to the Pentagon to meet with Defense Secretary Lloyd Austin, an impressive man of incredible service to our country whom I'd only ever seen on-screen. He was bigger in real life—more powerful in stature and more impressive in nature.

We sat around a conference table. After a brief introduction, each family member once again shared their story. He listened intently and answered each person with thought and empathy, directly addressing them.

Across the room I looked at Aviva, who had just shared the story of her own experience as a hostage. I told Secretary Austin that she and Abigail were from the same community and that, on the fifty-first day after Abigail's parents were murdered and she was taken hostage, they were freed from Gaza together. I told him that he had played an important part in Aviva and Abigail's freedom.

I watched as another big, powerful man wiped tears from his eyes.

That afternoon, I headed to the Capitol for Netanyahu's speech. The place had the feeling of a State of the Union address—a definitive, hour-long pronouncement on world affairs punctuated with frequent and seemingly bipartisan applause. That was partly an illusion: seventy Democrats skipped the speech, including Nancy Pelosi, who met with hostage families instead. In the gallery, Capitol Police arrested six Israelis—cousins and siblings of hostages—who stood up during one of Bibi's many ovations and revealed yellow shirts with the words "SEAL THE DEAL NOW," urging the Israeli prime minister to sign a deal with Hamas to bring the hostages home.

In a clear and forceful speech, Netanyahu argued that the current war with Hamas was a clash between civilization and barbarism, a fellow democracy's struggle for freedom against hateful, tyrannical ideologies. The speech was titled "Total Victory," and in it he asserted that the only possible definition of the term was the complete defeat and wiping out of Hamas—which must take place in order for Israel to be secure. He named Iran as the head of the octopus whose tentacles of hate were all around Israel. He spoke powerfully about Israel and the US's close relationship and the importance of our two democracies.

With gravitas and charm, he both cogently explained and forcefully condemned the noxious rise in anti-Semitism around the world—particularly on American college campuses, where so many Jewish students had come to feel embattled and isolated, and sometimes in physical danger. He spoke just as lucidly about the pro-Hamas rioters who had come out in full force on global streets, protesting not for democracy or freedom but in support of anarchy and terror. As if to illustrate his point, a few blocks away, pro-Hamas protesters took down the American flags in front of Union Station and burned them, hoisting Palestinian flags in their place. Then they painted ominous graffiti on the face of the Christopher Columbus Memorial Fountain in red: "Hamas is coming."

Shortly after, I attended Speaker Johnson's reception with the prime minister and his wife. I spoke with Noa Argamani, who had been rescued a month before. She is a kind young woman who was dancing in the desert air at a music festival with her boyfriend, only to become one of the most widely recognized faces of the day's horrors, when Hamas GoPros caught her being kidnapped on a motorcycle. She wanted to help us fight for the freedom of the hostages, including her boyfriend still in Gaza, but she had no idea where to start.

The prime minister is a careful speaker, but not so careful that I couldn't notice what he *didn't* say in his speech.

He did not say anything about a hostage deal. In fact, he said very little about the hostages at all. He did not ask his audience to empathize with their suffering or draw attention to how it might be relieved. I watched many people stand each time he said something in support of Israel, but I also noticed many middle-of-the-road leaders—people who had landed on the position that, even if they couldn't wholeheartedly support Israel's war effort, they could at least work for the release of the hostages—awkwardly trying to balance their reactions. A speech in such a prominent context, watched by so many around the world, was an unmatched opportunity to call attention to the plight of the hostages. That he did not do so felt like an abject failure.

***

The next day, I was back in the White House.

This time, I was sitting at a conference table with President Biden, Prime Minister Netanyahu, their high-level aides, and the other family members of American hostages. Biden was free of the burden of having to run for president again: just a few days before, after calls from leaders in his party to step aside, he had sent the people of America a letter that said:

> *It has been the greatest honor of my life to serve as your President. And while it has been my intention to seek reelection, I believe it is in the best interest of my party and the country for me to stand down and to focus solely on fulfilling my duties as President for the remainder of my term.*

He passed the torch to his vice president, Kamala Harris.

In this meeting, Biden spoke quietly and began by saying he felt the pain of the people in the room, sharing the stories of his own losses. Netanyahu spoke of the loss of his brother. It was affecting to hear both leaders begin the discussion on a personal note.

Jon Polin, Hersh's father, spoke next. He thanked both men before asking about the hostage release–ceasefire deal that we all understood was still being worked on behind the scenes by the US, Israel, Qatar, Egypt, and Hamas. This was the same deal that President Biden had laid out in a speech on May 31, two months earlier. Both Israel and Hamas had agreed to the framework of this deal over the last couple of months. We understood there were still issues to negotiate, but they were not insurmountable. If there was the political will from both sides, a deal could be finalized and signed. Jon was asking if this was a deal that Israel was ready to accept.

The president gave a general answer, as did the prime minister. Hostage families were looking for more. They were not going to get it.

Aviva, a hostage for fifty-one days, was in tears as she told the president and prime minister that they weren't doing enough to free her husband, Keith. Other family members started to cry as well.

The room was silent. It felt like minutes passed. It was a heavy, low moment.

I realized that, for the second time in three days, I had no choice but to tell the prime minister of Israel face-to-face what I really thought.

"Israelis are in trauma. The hostages need to come home to their families so that all of Israel can begin to heal," I said. "Until then, the country is sick. It cannot move forward." Netanyahu looked me in the eye, like he was scanning me for sources of weakness. Biden just looked down. I could sense his frustration with all of this.

I went on. I told them both that they were not doing enough, and that in this time that demanded bold leadership, hostages' lives depended on them.

I glanced at the president who was shaking his head in agreement. I looked at the prime minister who was still looking right at me, emotionless.

I continued speaking directly with these two leaders. I said to the president that we needed him to keep leading the efforts and do more, and to the prime minister, I made it clear that he was the only one who could make the deal from the Israeli side. This was the time. I then directly asked both of these men for their commitment to bring our loved ones home.

I first looked to President Biden, who said he would work for the rapid release of all the hostages. Then I looked at Prime Minister Netanyahu. He said, glancing at Biden: "The same as the president."

I looked right into the prime minister's eyes and spoke. "We are all watching, and we are counting the days," I said. "The hostages cannot wait another day. They need to come home now."

In the days Prime Minister Netanyahu was in D.C., we learned of five more hostages who had been taken alive on October 7 and were pronounced dead.

As for Biden, the hostages were a defining challenge in a long public life—one of his last big, achievable goals that hovered tantalizingly in the near distance. I knew that he wouldn't consider his work complete if he left office with the hostages still in Gaza, but I also knew he hadn't yet been able to make the world turn the way he wanted it to.

***

As I write this, 111 hostages—children, women, and men—still languish in dark rooms and tunnels, without enough food or even air, as the war continues to rage around them, and their odds of survival grow narrower.

Eight Americans are still held hostage in Gaza: Edan Alexander, twenty; Sagui Dekel-Chen, thirty-five; Hersh Goldberg Polin, twenty-three; Omer Neutra, twenty-two; Keith Siegel, sixty-five; and we know that three of our Americans were killed on October 7 and their bodies were brought to Gaza as hostages: Itay Chen, twenty; Judih Weinstein, seventy; and Gadi Haggai, seventy-three.

Their plight is only one element of a bottomless human tragedy. Nearly two million Palestinians and over 250,000 Israelis have been chased from their homes across ten inconclusive months of fighting. The war Hamas began on October 7 is by far the deadliest individual round of fighting in the Israeli-Arab conflict. Over 1,600 Israelis have been killed since October 7—more than in the entire Second Intifada. Israel has killed an estimated sixteen thousand Hamas terrorists, along with thousands of innocent Palestinian civilians.

Israel is a place without easy answers, which can frustrate and even anger people who look at the difficulties she faces from far away. The attack, the war, the hostage standoff, and a slow-boiling domestic political crisis in Israel amount to a society-wide psychic wound, the full extent of which can only really begin to be understood in the long run, over the course of years and decades. Many Israelis see the post–October 7 period as their second war of independence, an existential struggle for the Israeli state in the Jewish people's ancient homeland. Many others see the fate of the hostages as the real test, as a barometer for the values of the country in which they live.

The Israeli outlook remains positive for me, a conclusion that I base largely on the experience of my own family. Michael, Amalia, and Abigail have a loving new home. Leron lost her sister on October 7, and then she and Zoli took in her nieces and nephew without ever stopping to think about it.

The Israeli tendency to fiercely embrace life over death is not without its dark side, though. Shlomit has cared for her grandchildren with such love and intensity that I sometimes worry whether she's ever taken any time to really mourn Smadar. In a similar way, life has moved so quickly for Abigail and her siblings that the pain sometimes shows itself with an eerie subtlety.

Hagar and her family are still figuring out where their new life will be, far away from their destroyed paradise on the Gaza border. The other residents of Kfar Aza are long-term temporary guests of a kibbutz in the middle of the country. Each and every one of them knows someone who was murdered, kidnapped, or raped—sixty-three people were killed and ten kidnapped from Kfar Aza that day. Five of their neighbors are still hostages in Gaza: Keith Siegel, sixty-five; twins Gali and Ziv Berman, twenty-six; and two young women, British Israeli Emily Damari, who is twenty-seven, and Doron Steinbrecher, thirty.

This is the shared story of Israel after October 7.

When I look at Michael, Amalia, and Abigail, I see a miniature version of a bigger picture. Abigail lived through nearly two months as a hostage; Michael and Amalia, fourteen hours hidden in a closet, after these three little children watched their parents be murdered by Hamas. They are wounded but not defeated. They carry scars no one else will be able to see, but they will take their lives back. The children are all different ages—they will all have different memories of their parents, and each will have a different relationship to them.

My message for the world is the same now as it was in the immediate aftermath of the attack: No amount of fighting, no Israeli battlefield achievements or Hamas duplicity, has changed my basic outlook. The sides must make a deal that brings home the hostages, stops the fighting, and allows humanitarian aid to reach the vulnerable people in Gaza who need it. No child should be a hostage and no child should be the victim of war. This tragedy doesn't need to get any worse than it already is: if Hamas released the people it stole on October 7, the war would end.

This story ends with a gaping lack of conclusion, a chaos of ongoing death and destruction. But it also ends with Abigail safe with her siblings and in the arms of people who love her.

Her return contains an even greater hope, which is that a better reality can indeed exist on the other side of so much suffering.

Saving Abigail taught me that we can help make that better reality possible, even if we can't solve every problem ourselves. You just go and do what you can, give what you can, and make sure your efforts are filled with love and hope and warmth, no matter how impossible or dark the situation may seem.

Today, when I look at the photo of Abigail, copies of which I printed and handed out by the thousands, and which wound up on the desk of the president of the United States, I don't think as much about the massacre she survived, or the murder of her parents, or the atrocity of her kidnapping. I think about the life that she'll have, and the better country and world that I hope she'll live in. I feel grateful, even amazed, by the certainty that she'll be known as someone other than a victim of terrorism.

My hope is that Abigail will show us all the dimensions of a life beyond this singular tragedy. What I know for sure is that right now, this very second, she's giving us all something to look forward to.

EPILOGUE

SEPTEMBER 1, 2024

On August 21, 2024, tears streamed down my face as I stood backstage watching Rachel Goldberg and Jon Polin, the parents of twenty-three-year-old American hostage Hersh Goldberg-Polin, speaking onstage at the Democratic National Convention.

As they walked up and stood at the podium, all of the attendees gave a prolonged standing ovation. Before Rachel and Jon said a single word, a chant rose loudly and powerfully throughout United Center: "BRING THEM HOME."

Rachel, who has displayed superhuman resolve and composure for almost a year since her son was badly injured and forcefully taken from the Nova music festival, was overcome by this reception, and she bent over in tears. When she collected herself, her voice rang out clearly: "At this moment, one hundred and nine treasured human beings are being held hostage by Hamas in Gaza. They are Christians, Jews, Muslims, Hindus, and Buddhists. They are from twenty-three different countries.

Among the hostages are eight American citizens. One of those Americans is our only son, Hersh."

As she spoke, the arena was silent. I looked at the crowd, observing the pained faces of the diverse men and women in the audience on the multiple screens in front of me: one man with his hands in prayer and tears in his eyes, some had yellow hostage ribbon pins fastened to their suit jackets, others were wrapped in Palestinian keffiyeh—everyone remained standing, teary-eyed, holding onto each word.

Many feared there would be shouts of protest; instead, there was an outpouring of love, warmth, and empathy. Much like at the Republican National Convention one month earlier, I was deeply moved by the reaction of my fellow Americans and the heart with which they responded to our call for the immediate release of all the hostages and an end to the fighting. They understood these were real people and they needed to return to their families.

"This is a political convention," Jon said. "But needing our son, and all the hostages home, is not a political issue. It is a humanitarian issue." He continued, "There is a surplus of agony on all sides of the tragic conflict in the Middle East. In a competition of pain, there are no winners." The audience, still on its feet, erupted into applause.

Rachel ended by addressing her son: "Hersh, Hersh, if you can hear us, WE LOVE YOU. STAY STRONG. SURVIVE."

In the last days of August, Hersh and five other young people were murdered by Hamas in a tunnel under Rafah in southern Gaza.

***

As I write these words, it has been 330 days since our loved ones were taken. While US, Qatari, and Egyptian leaders are working around the clock to release the hostages and end the fighting and suffering, there are two men—Benjamin Netanyahu and Yahya Sinwar—whose motives have an enormous impact on whether a life-saving deal is signed.

Yet since October 7, when we woke up into a living nightmare, we have fought tirelessly for the lives of our loved ones, giving a voice to their humanity and the humanity of all the people in the region—while finding boundless compassion in others and holding firmly onto our own.

It is our choice to act. What we all say and do matters.

Hersh and many others could have and should have been saved. For those who are still alive, time is running out.

ACKNOWLEDGMENTS

This story honors the lives of 1,200 innocent babies, children, men, and women murdered on October 7, and the 246 people taken hostage that day. I am most grateful to so many people for their love and support on this journey.

To the American hostage families—Yael and Adi Alexander; Yehuda Beinin; Hagit and Ruby Chen; Gillian Kaye and Jonathan Dekel-Chen; Rachel Goldberg and Jon Polin; Orna and Ronen Neutra; Aviva, Lucy, Elan, Lee, Emily, and Hanna Siegel; Andrea Weinstein and Iris Weinstein Haggai: I wish as I write this book that your loved ones—Edan, Itay, Sagui, Hersh, Omer, Keith, Judy, and Gadi—are all back with you. I never imagined over three hundred days would pass and they would still be in Gaza. For ten months, you have been brave and tireless, fighting with heart and passion, doing everything possible to hug and hold them again. I love you all.

Will Murphy: Thank you for your vision, your heart, and believing in the importance of sharing this story. Armin Rosen: You listened and then taught me more than I could have imagined. I am most grateful. David Samuels and Alana Newhouse: Thank you for sharing your hearts and this journey with me.

Anthony Ziccardi: Your energy and passion inspire me. Thank you to Michael Wilson, Maddie Sturgeon, and all the team at Post Hill Press for helping me to publish this book with thought and speed.

Jen Seelig and Lynda Dorf: I could not have done this without you. You are two extraordinary women whom I am blessed to call friends and colleagues. Jenny Gallagher, I am so happy you joined our team.

Jessica Bernton, Huston Harris, Jacob Kwasman, Thomas Zier, Rebecca Klein, Jeremy Margolies, Belle Yoeli, Marcia Bronstein, Julie Rayman, and everyone at AJC: Your knowledge, professionalism, and huge hearts created meetings and opportunities for hostage families in D.C. Jill Zuckman, Kendra Barkoff Lamy, Jade Klain, Mariel Saez, Sarah Mucha, Molly Salter, Alex Russo, Aoife McCarthy, Dakar Jose Lanzino, and all at SKDK: I know how hard you have worked and continue to work for the release of our loved ones and to support our families along the way. You have been incredible, caring partners. Gefen Ahituv: I dream that more leaders in Israel could have your pragmatism, kindness, and empathy. Wholehearted thank-you to David Gilette, William Daroff, Jeremy Bash, Tom Nides, and all who have been advising and supporting the American hostage families from day one.

Jon Adrabi: Thank you for calling me when I was down and opening a world of possibilities. Bar Ben Yaakov and Matan Sivek: I admire your relentless efforts to release all of the hostages. Anthony Welcher, Brette Powell, Dan Berman, Virginia Beckett, and the RNC team: Thank you for your kindness and for giving an important platform to the hostage families' stories. Keith Fernandez, Lindsay Holst, Lisa Geers, Minyon Moore,

Shailagh Murray, Stephanie Cutter and Stephen Krupin, and the DNC team: Thank you for helping to elevate the story of our eight American hostages being held in Gaza.

I am deeply grateful for the informal schooling I was given generously from unexpected teachers, who helped to open my eyes to a world I never wanted to be a part of but needed to learn to navigate—quickly. Roger Carstens: From the first time we spoke, you told me I could call you twenty-four-seven. I have done so many times for advice, and sometimes just because hearing your voice gave me hope and strength. Mickey Bergman: You scared me in the beginning because I wasn't prepared for what you knew. Since then, I have learned how truly special you are, and I am grateful for your moral and strategic clarity. Robert Satloff: In one afternoon you set me straight about a world you have spent many years mastering. Eytan Stibbe: You traveled to where few have gone and shared one of these adventures to Doha with us out of kindness and determination to help.

Thank you to my dearest friends whose love and care I have needed more than ever. Jeff Larivee: From the moment I returned from Israel in October, you have fed me and supported me. Marci Foster: Thank you for always checking to see where in the world I was and how I was holding up. Adam Schiff: My parents were right, you are special. Karen Sachs: You helped me find strength in the hardest moments. Wendy Greuel: Your "Just checking on you my friend" always came at the right time. Ellyn Lindsay: You make me smile. Sharon Brous and Melissa Balaban: I appreciate your love and friendship. Anthony Mercurio: No matter where in the world, you've been there for me. Amanda Silverman: You know when to reach out and make me feel better. Dana and Matt Walden: Thankful for all your love and support.

Janet and Barry Lang: You are inspiring people who show up in quiet and considerate ways. Doron Algam: You are always there to make life easier and kinder. Nicole Mutchnik: I am grateful for your grace and goodness. Corinne and Dan Goldman: Thank you and your beautiful children for your friendship and love. Nick and Nancy Frankel: You are two true guardian angels who came to help protect and care for Leron and Zoli and their six children. Jon Davidson: You always help in special ways. Kay Sides: We've been blessed to raise our kids and ourselves together. Stephanie Daily Smith: I am happy to always be on your team. Sheryl Weissberg: Lucky me, you are my big sister always. Sybil Robson Orr and Matthew Orr: Thank you for believing in me and checking on me from all over the world. Christine and Nancy Pelosi: From October 7, you were there, sharing our family's story the next morning and condemning the terror. You have continued to show incredible love and support for Abigail and all the hostages.

I am forever grateful to many other friends and supporters for your kindness, help, and hugs: Abbey Onn, Alexandra McPeak, Alex Sussman, Alexi Rosenfeld, Amy Strauss, Annabelle Rutledge, Andrea Aberger, Anya Wareck, Arpita Diamond, Ashleigh Lancaster, Asif Mahmood, Avery Siegel, Barbi Brodus, Beau Goodman, Blair Berk, Brian Diamond, Brian Pryzbylski, Capricia Marshall, Cara Fano, Chris Korge, Cindy Persky, Claire Lucas, Cortez Winston, Courtney La Bau, Crystal Spain, Dan Auerbach, Daniel Inlender, Daniella Foux, David Weber, Dean Shram, Deborah Marcus, Diane Levin, Diego Lamboglia, Drew Foster, Elad Oz, Elizabeth Tauro, Emily Berret, Enedina

Jimenez, Eitan Teiger, Ethan Sander, Etienne Maurice, Gaya Bing, Gita Bendheim, Graziella Cappelletti, Greg Silverman, Halle Sasse, Herbert Block, Hyma Moore, Jack Miller, Jaime Dominguez, Jake Delaney, Jaime Harrison, Jamie Amos, Jane Wong, Janet Lonner, Jen Mallan, Jen S. Newsom, Jenny Biggs, Jessie Chipps, Joel Roth, John Emerson, Jon Levin, Josh Weinberg, Judy Dlugacz, Karen Bass, Kimberly Marteau Emerson, Laura Schuman, Lee Dugger, Lesley Weiss, Lior Temkin, Lis Jimenez, Liz Gilbert, Marcia Riklis, Mariola Barczewska, Marsha Laufer, Michael Marquardt, Mike Smith, Mo Butler, Nancy Berman, Nancy Carell, Nancy Greenstein, Nancy Kauffman, Nancy Remar, Nate Shutman, Nati Kaspin, Nema Mansouri, Nikola Otlans, Nina Tassler, Oren Knapp, Patrick Kennedy, Peter Alexander, Rani Kaspin, Rebecca Brindza, Rich Henick, Rivka Elbert, Rob Mallan, Robert Warren, Ron Huldai, Ruthie Berber, Sam Cornale, Sarah Fitzpatrick, Sarah McBride, Shalom Elbert, Shayne Lipsey, Silvio Eisenberg, Star Jones, Susan Berger, Susan Boster, Sydney Brown, Sydney Stracher, Teena Hostevitch, Terri New, Thomas Shram, Ti Aguirre, Tommy Rodriguez, Tracy Boher, Victor Herlinksy, Wendy Klein, Will Rollins, and Yigal Gal.

The following people shared so much kindness and helped me in ways I never could have imagined needing. Huma Abedin: In early critical moments when I needed a life line, you reached out to help. Ben Sherwood: After many years, you came back into my life and reminded me in my darkest moments of that fearless teenager who still lives inside me. Jay Footlik: From breakfasts in D.C. to Doha, and against all of the odds, you make the impossible happen and with a huge heart. Sophia Abrams: You called when I was lost, literally took my hand and set me off on this journey, and continued to be there for me and others. Penny Nance: You have been kind and bright every day since we met on the Hill and have guided me in an unknown world. To the Qatari leadership: You helped bring Abigail back to our family; you met with us hostage families and continue to work tirelessly to bring everyone home.

Hillary Clinton: No matter the hour or where in the world I have found you, you made time to be there for me. Your grace and grit have given me power and purpose in dark moments. Cory Booker: Sharing Simcha Torah in Jerusalem on October 6 and supporting each other throughout the following days' tragic attack bonded us in a life-changing way. Thank you for your friendship on really tough days, and for agreeing that grasshoppers will stop neither of us. Veronica Duran, Sam Schifrin, Stephan Suric, Hanna Mori, Anne Sciano, Mather Martin, Samantha Maltzman, and my hero Kevin Batts: you have become like family to me, and I am deeply grateful for your support and love.

The secret to getting things done on the Hill is knowing the most important people—the staff. Since October 7, I have met so many incredible staffers, and I wish I could name them all. I am thankful to all of you for your vital help to arrange meetings and navigate maze-like capital buildings. Gideon Bragin: I am grateful for your wisdom and kindness. Wayne Williams: You appeared at times when I needed a hug, heart, and hope. Ryan Alban: Thank you for your consistent help and support. Shir Attias: You have been steady and kind in very turbulent times and kept it real with all of us. Daniel Bleiberg: Your insight and leadership have been invaluable in helping me navigate uncharted, painful times. Eric Trager: Thank you for all your acuity and wisdom. Dennis Wischmeier: I appreciate your help very much. Adam Koslovski: From D.C. to Tel Aviv, your help, friendship, and support of hostage families has been invaluable. Elisa Catalano Ewers: You have been an unwavering friend, thought partner, and powerful advocate for the hostages and for peace in the Middle East.

I am thankful to the many leaders I have met on both sides of the aisle who are all committed to getting every one of our loved ones back from Gaza. Leader Hakeem Jeffries and Leader Steve Scalise: The history books will show that you each met with hostage families and made releasing the hostages a priority and a bipartisan commitment. Thank you. Joni Ernst: You have been a warrior for the American hostages and are working on so many levels to make Hamas let them go. Kirsten Gillibrand: You were one of the first senators to take a poster to the Senate floor with Abigail's face and share her story. Ritchie Torres: You speak truth and share hope. Chris Coons: You have been a voice of reason and steadiness and answered my calls compassionately. Zoe Lofgren: Thank you for being a voice of reason from day one. Mike Lawler: Your partnership and commitment to hostage release has been reassuring. Josh Gottheimer: You are a true mensch. Lindsey Graham: Early on, you shared your vision of the Middle East and your commitment to rescuing the hostages. Haley Stevens: Being your guest at the State of the Union was an honor, and your dedication to the release of American hostages in Gaza and around the world is inspiring. Jacky Rosen: I still hear your voice from our phone call on the night of October 7, and you continue to be a voice of clarity and strength for me and so many others. Susan Collins: Your compassion and love for Abigail made all of the difference in the world, and to this day, you continue to speak out for all of the hostages. Thank you.

Thank you to all leaders on both sides of the aisle, especially those I met with multiple times:

Leader Chuck Schumer, Senators Alex Padilla, Angus King, Ben Cardin, Bernie Sanders, Bob Casey, Chris Murphy, Cindy Hyde-Smith, Elizabeth Warren, James Lankford, Jon Fetterman, Jon Ossoff, Katie Britt, Lephonza Butler, Lisa Murkowski, Marco Rubio, Mark Kelly, Mark Warner, Markwayne Mullin, Marsha Blackburn, Richard Blumenthal, Shelley Moore Capito, Sherrod Brown, Tammy Baldwin, Tammy Duckworth, Ted Budd, Thom Tillis, and Tim Kaine. House Committee on Foreign Affairs Chair Mike McCaul and Ranking Member Greg Meeks, Representatives Ann Wagner, Ashley Hinson, Becca Balint, Colin Allred, Darrell Issa, Debbie Wasserman Schultz, Donald Norcross, Elissa Slotkin, Eric Swalwell, Greg Landsman, Jamaal Bowman, Jamie Raskin, Jasmine Crocket, Jeff Jackson, Jimmy Panetta, Kathy Manning, Kim Schrier, Lisa Blunt-Rochester, Mariannette Miller-Meeks, Pramila Jayapal, Ruben Gallego, Steny Hoyer, Summer Lee, Sydney Kamlager-Dove, and Ted Lieu.

The United States government worked nonstop since October 7 for Abigail and 104 children and women to be released from Gaza at the end of November 2023, and it continues its stoic and steadfast stewardship and determination to get the rest of the hostages out of Gaza. Deputy Secretary of the Treasury Wally Adeyemo, Attorney General Merrick Garland, Defense Secretary Lloyd Austin, and your teams, thank you for meeting with us and helping us. Ambassador Jack Lew: Thank you for showing up and caring. Ambassador Timmy Davis: Thank you for meeting and helping us in Doha. Steve Gillen: Thank you for your help and guidance in Israel with our family and for embracing us meaningfully in hard times. Chandler Yonge: You jumped in and did not miss a beat. Lisa Skolnick: You have been advising and coordinating hostage families with heart and humility. Bill Burns: You and your team have met with the American hostage families, and you have traveled nonstop to and from the region engaging with all the players to release Abigail and our loved ones. Thank you. Roger Carstens, Charlotte Nazarian, Rob Crotty, Elizabeth Tabron, and all your SPEHA team: Your tireless and often thankless work to release American hostages saves lives and helped bring Abigail home. I am forever thankful. Antony Blinken: I am grateful for your steady strength and indefatigable efforts. After our meetings with you in Israel, I watched you go outside to hug and hold Israeli hostage families, demonstrating that despite the complexities of your work, showing human compassion can be simple. Brett McGurk: Watching you push Abigail on the White House swing is a symbol of your tireless diplomatic push to bring her and most of the children back at the end of November 2023. Keep pushing. David Cotter: You always called back, listened carefully, and shared what you could; and you continually reaffirmed the government's commitment to releasing the hostages. Jake Sullivan: After many straightforward, honest, and truly hard meetings with you and your National Security Council team, my respect and admiration for you only grows. There's no one I would rather have fighting in the trenches for the life of a three-year-old American child than you.

I have learned that the White House teams are made up of kind and hard-working individuals. Thank you to Adam

Schultz, Annie Tomasini, Anthony Bernal, Kate Waters, Camilo Haller, Carly Faulkner, Charlie Fromstein, Connor Goddard, Dean Lieberman, Dennis Cheng, Erin Wilson, Evelyn Larsen, John Scanlon, Lorraine Voles, Phil Gordon, Rebecca Lissner, Wayne Skinner, and all of your colleagues. A special thank-you to whoever bakes the chocolate chip cookies.

Vice President Harris: When you and the second gentleman surprised the American hostage families at the State Department a couple of weeks after October 7, you showed us how much these kidnapped Americans meant to you personally. Thank you for your tireless partnership with President Biden to release all of the hostages and bring an end to the fighting.

President Biden: Thank you for your moral clarity and for demonstrating what it means to be an exceptional leader. I shudder to think where Abigail and the 104 women and children released at the end of November would be today were it not for you. I know you will not rest until all of our loved ones return to their families.

My family is my northern star. Shula Benjamin: You and Yacov taught me about your rich Middle Eastern history and what it meant to be Jewish Arab refugees from a nation that did not want you. Adam, Jen, Pam, and Steven Hirsh: We live proudly as part of Anita and Stanley's legacy of Tikun Olam. Tenafly Families: Friday night dinners with the Alexanders have been a highlight at the end of difficult weeks. Speaking of food, Yotam Kaspin, my son-in-law, you have made sure we were fed and taken care of and have spent a lot of hours just being there in the most thoughtful ways. Dana Ben Ezra, Iris Shimonov, Lior Shachar, Nira Naftali, Rinat Horvat, Ruti Lederer, Sharon Berenshteen, and Tzipi Samra, my Israeli sisters: *todah rabah*.

Avihai Brodutch: You saved Abigail on October 7, and literally went to the ends of the earth, wearing a dress shirt, moving mountains to bring your family home.

Hagar Brodutch: For fifty-one days in unimaginable circumstances, you fought for the survival of your three children and Abigail, your dear friends Smadar and Roee's little girl. You are my hero.

Shlomit and Eitan: I close my eyes and still see us all sitting in your front yard, Eitan's paintings pouring out of his studio, Shabtai beaming, all of our children running around, and Shlomit caring for all of us. Shlomit: Through the heartbreaking tragedy of losing your incredible daughter and her husband and having your granddaughter kidnapped, you continue to take care of us all, especially your beautiful grandchildren.

Dori, Keren, Ron, Or, and Noam Breen: You are five very special people who I marvel at, am grateful for, and love to be with. Keren and Dori: You have shown an excellence in humanity I never knew possible, and I am in awe of how you held our family up and gave them the will and grace to move forward.

Zoli: I think about our conversations about fatherhood and how much it has always meant to you to be a good father. You are doing it. I see how beautifully you have raised your three amazing children and now embrace, love, and father your little nieces and nephew. You take care of all of these kids with warmth and clarity, and even on hard days, with a good dosage of humor and humility.

Leron, my beautiful niece: We have been friends and allies since you were a little girl, forming a special connection we have shared throughout the years. You took care of my children, a period we all fondly remember. As we continue to pick up the pieces, we support each other in the most meaningful ways. Smadar was killed trying to protect Abigail, Amalia, and Michael, and she will always be in your hearts and souls as you love, care for, and raise them.

Noa, Aaron, Eden, Kobe, and Talya: Through your love, you give me the strength to fight. I could not do what I do without you, and in many ways I do it for you. I love you all. Noa: Since I hugged you goodbye on October 8, you have been an incredible source of strength for our family and for me. Thank you for your resolute partnership in freeing Abigail and for sharing her story so heartfully even when it was so painful. You have made my work better and filled me with great pride.

Zohar, Inbar, Daniella, Michael, Amalia, and Abigail: You guys are the best. I love our long, loud, and fun playdates. There is never a dull moment being with you all, and I look forward to our time together, always. It inspires me to watch you take turns caring for each other, and I know that while it isn't always easy, you will continue to be each other's best friends. I love being your aunt, and I love you all.

Finally, thank you to all the people who were touched and moved by Abigail's story. Your outpouring of love from all over the world held me and our family up through fifty-one days of hell. Together, we succeeded in Saving Abigail.

Please keep the hostages and their families in your hearts until they are all free.

ABOUT THE AUTHOR

Liz Hirsh Naftali is the great-aunt of Abigail Mor Edan, a three-year-old who was held hostage in Gaza for fifty-one days. Abigail was kidnapped by Hamas terrorists on October 7, 2023, from her kibbutz, Kfar Aza, after her parents were both murdered in front of her by Hamas terrorists.

In the wake of that attack, Naftali became a fervent advocate working for the release of the hostages. Even after Abigail's release on November 26, she remains dedicated to working for all those who remain in captivity in Gaza.

Naftali is a businesswoman and the host and creator of *The Capitol Coffee Connection* podcast, a platform where she invites prominent, diverse leaders to talk about the common thread that binds us all together—our shared experiences, stories, and the very essence of our heart and humanity—leaving out politics and policy.

Naftali is the mother of five children and has lived between Israel and the US since 1992.

Made in the USA
Las Vegas, NV
14 October 2024

dff2f8d8-52ee-4b8d-8700-e0b649f86933R01